Dames Employées

The Feminization of Postal Work in Nineteenth-Century France

Dames Employées

The Feminization of Postal Work in Nineteenth-Century France

Susan Bachrach

Copublished by
The Institute for Research in History and The Haworth Press, Inc.

Dames Employées: *The Feminization of Postal Work in Nineteenth-Century France* has also been published as *Women & History,* Number 8, Winter 1983.

Library of Congress Cataloging in Publication Data

Bachrach, Susan.
      Dames employées.
      (Women & history; no. 8)
      Bibliography: p.
      Includes index.
      1. Postal service—France—Employees—History—19th century.
2. Women—Employment—France—History—19th century. I. Title. II. Series.
HE6989.P4B33 1984   331.4'813834944   83-22879
ISBN 0-86656-205-2

About the Author

Susan Bachrach received her PhD from the University of Wisconsin-Madison in 1981. She is presently completing her second year as a post-doctoral fellow in the interdisciplinary Women and Work program at the Graduate Center, City University of New York. She also teaches at Queens College, and is a member of the Institute for Research in History.

Dames Employées:
The Feminization of Postal Work in Nineteenth-Century France

Women & History
Number 8

CONTENTS

Acknowledgments

Most of the research for this book was done in France at the Archives Nationales, the Bibliothèque Nationale, the Ministère des Postes et des Télécommunications, the Musée de la Poste, and several departmental and municipal archives. The staffs at the libraries of the Ministère des Postes and the Musée de la Poste were especially helpful, and I am very grateful for their warm cooperation. I would also like to thank M. Félice, then director of personnel at the ministry, and his staff for their extraordinary assistance in making available records which had not yet been deposited in the archives.

Major financial support for this study was provided by a French-American Foundation Tocqueville fellowship. Preparation of the manuscript was aided by the Women and Work Program at the Graduate Center of the City University of New York, under National Institute of Mental Health grant 44/495.

Several friends and teachers have helped me during various stages of this project. I would like to thank, first, my husband, Peter D. Bachrach. He provided research help and amiable company in the dull work of collecting quantifiable data, and his interest and advice sustained me throughout the research and writing. The thesis on which this study is based was written under the supervision of Harvey Goldberg, from whom I also received my initial training as a social historian. His concern that historians communicate in a language shared by those outside academe and that historians strive to reach a wider public will always remain with me. Edward Gargan and John Sharpless both helped shape my thinking on the topic. Theresa McBride's assistance in steering me through the morass of occupational coding is much appreciated. Joan Scott's enthusiastic interest in this subject and her advice and critical comments at every stage of the research and writing have been especially valuable. She provided a fine model for an apprentice scholar, and I owe her my deepest gratitude.

Introduction

In western Europe and the United States the late nineteenth century represents an important transitional period in the history of women's work. In nineteenth-century cities the major employers of women were households hiring servants and the garment and textile industries. Toward the end of the century, however, women began to enter new fields of employment; it was during this period of relatively rapid commercial and industrial growth that women first entered clerical jobs in government bureaucracies and the offices of private businesses. Female clerks were clearly novelties in these settings, where formerly only men had worked. But women were there to stay and their numbers kept growing. In advanced industrialized societies today more women work in offices than in either industrial, domestic, or agricultural settings, and women greatly outnumber men in clerical fields.

Viewing the expansion of women's employment in clerical fields over the last century, social scientists have regarded this so-called "feminization of the service sector" as an inevitable trend in the development of industrializing societies. Writers may have disagreed about the significance of the change for women, some having argued, on the positive side, that clerical jobs offered a social respectability and security of employment that few female wage-earners had previously enjoyed, while others have pointed more critically to the low wages and dead-end character of clerical work. Most recent descriptions have generally agreed, however, that it was the steady growth of clerical jobs which created the demand for a relatively cheap, plentiful supply of labor and that women were available in more than sufficient numbers to meet that demand. Improvements in girls' schooling, beginning in the late nineteenth century, swelled the numbers of educated women and continuing progress in education assured that the pool of women always expanded faster than available clerical positions.[1]

Still, when I began this study, little beyond such generalities and opinions was actually known about women's initial entrance into clerical work. The historical literature on the subject was almost non-existent.[2] Many questions needed to be answered. First, from the viewpoint of the individual employer, what were the specific pressures, economic or otherwise, that persuaded or, perhaps, forced him to hire women, and hire them when he did rather than earlier or later? What were the exact events surrounding the first appearance of women in his work place? Second, from the perspective of the employees, what were the backgrounds of the women seeking clerical employment and why did they desire to enter the new field of work? Were they "middle-class" women leaving home in an effort to find self-fulfillment and independence, as some writers claimed? Or were they women from working-class families desiring to escape such traditional female jobs as seamstress or servant?

Answers to these questions required focusing on a specific work setting, and the feminization of French postal services seemed a good choice for several reasons. At the turn of the century the Postal Administration was the largest single employer of women in clerical jobs in France. Aggregate census statistics revealed a steady increase in women employed in the postal service. As every specialist of French social history knows, references to the *postières*—female postal employees—are common in general histories, as writers have identified postal employment as one of the few avenues of social mobility for women besides schoolteaching (although no one had ever documented the phenomenon).[3] Employed in jobs where they could use their educations and which conferred the status of civil servant, *postières* were considered "ladies" and enjoyed a social respectability unknown to most working women. Sainte-Beuve was the first of a line of authors who have portrayed the *postière* as a romantic heroine; his novelette *Christel* (1844) tells the story of one of the early female post office managers—our equivalent of postmistresses—who antedated by many decades the first generation of urban postal employees.[4]

The feminization of postal work in France assumed additional interest when I learned from an early study written by Jeanne Bouvier that postal administrators had decided in 1892 to hire *dames employées*—lady clerks—to work in post offices in Paris and other major cities. No women had ever worked in these clerical positions before. Yet according to Bouvier's account, the Postal Administration had employed women earlier as rural post office managers and had also hired women in the fifteen years preceding 1892 to work in urban offices as telegraph and telephone operators and in central administrative offices as clerks and copyists. Traditionalists initially raised objections to women's employment in these jobs, and certain prejudices persisted throughout the period before the war. Nevertheless, the placement of women in these areas had generally proceeded without strong objections being voiced, either by supervisors, male employees, or the general public. In contrast, representatives of all three groups protested vociferously when women first appeared as Parisian post office clerks in 1892. The variety of jobs women filled in the Postal Administration, the difference in the timing of their entrance into these jobs, and the varying character of the reaction to their employment suggested the possibility for a comparative analysis which would illuminate the larger process of the feminization of clerical jobs.[5]

Finally, that the Postal Administration was a government agency and its policy-making process relatively visible greatly heightened my chances of finding sufficient documentation on the feminization of jobs. A variety of source materials—administrative and legislative reports, personnel yearbooks, employee journals, some unpublished government records—would enable me to trace the postal employers' recruitment policies and the role played by legislators as well as male employees in shaping the hiring practices which differentiated men and women. An analysis of hundreds of individuals' employment records linked with birth documents and other civil records would provide information on the social backgrounds and employment patterns of the female employees compared to the men they were joining. Because the Postal Administration was highly centralized, recruitment and other employee policies affected all France and the focus of the study would therefore be national; at the same time, however, the presence of central offices and the high concentration of postal employees in Paris would require heeding particular attention to the capital.

I found, not unexpectedly, that while women working in postal services were in certain respects privileged female wage-earners, they still experienced many of the same kinds of discriminatory treatment universally characterizing the position of women in the French economy. The state offered no model of sexual equality. This should not be surprising considering that French leaders paid little attention to economic and social inequalities of any kind in an age when privileged laissez-faire capitalism was triumphant. It is important to remember, moreover, that French law in the nineteenth century reinforced male dominance by severely limiting women's civil and political rights.[6] Mirroring their formally inscribed difference from and inferiority to men, women in the Postal Administration were segregated into a special female grade and usually worked in predominantly female work groups. They received lower wages than male clerks even when they did exactly the same work. And although some women had opportunities for advancement, the positions open to them were in designated female grades; they were denied access to the career ladder up which male clerks climbed.

In this context, it is important to point out that the function women played in filling low-level positions in the administrative hierarchy and, at the same time, not competing with men for higher-level posts proved vital. In an era when competition for promotions among a steadily growing number of low-level male employees was producing serious morale problems, threatening social peace in the work place, and discouraging more qualified men from seeking employment in the administration, the employment of women—denied real promotions—could reduce the competition for men. Yet, the men employed in the Postal Administration usually perceived women only as competitors. The important point to stress here is that the advantages of employing women went beyond their relative cheapness and availability.

Indeed, while women's subordinate status in the clerical work force in France in this period fit with my understanding of the history of women's wage work, the more I contemplated the advantages women offered the individual employer, the more problematic I found previous interpretations of the feminization of clerical jobs. All that I had read suggested that women rapidly entered expanding clerical fields as plentiful, cheap labor. Yet what struck me in this instance was the resistance women kept encountering. If women offered the employer so many advantages and were available to work in large numbers, why was the feminization of jobs as slow and selective as it appears to have been? Importantly, why did the Postal Administration wait until 1892 to hire women as post office clerks when it had recruited women much earlier for other positions in the administration?

Obviously there were limits to the feminization of jobs imposed by considerations other than simply financial ones. Thus, I began to look much more closely for evidence of how these limits were defined, to search for specific historical conditions which had facilitated women's entrance into the work force and, equally important, those conditions—often ignored owing to the common tendency to look at where women are rather then where they are not—which had hindered the hiring of women. Despite the current fashionability of emphasizing the importance that women's role in the family plays in shaping job segregation by sex, this case reaffirmed my belief in the dominant importance of external factors.[7] For example, the tendency of women to move in and out of the work force as their family responsibilities and needs shift over time is supposed to have prejudiced employers, particularly those who needed a more stable work force, against employing women. Yet, despite real family responsibilities, women in the Postal Administration had low turnover rates because of the way the employment was structured: in addition to such incentives to remain in the work force as salary raises and pensions, there was no "marriage bar" as there was in England and many other countries, where women had little choice but to leave the work force upon marriage. In any case, any desire of the postal employer to reduce turnover would not explain why he hired women for certain clerical jobs and not others.

In this study I show that the weight of tradition was so great in maintaining definitions of "men's work" in the Postal Administration that employers broke with the old custom of hiring just men as post office clerks only after a conjuncture of events, a combination of circumstances, produced a crisis situation that left the administrators little choice. Behind any "tradition," of course, lies an integrated system of cultural attitudes and vested interests, and breaking tradition correspondingly threatens those attitudes and interests. In the case of the Postal Administration, the reaction to the feminization of urban clerking positions was so strong that after the crisis situation had subsided, women's employment as urban post office clerks failed to progress in a steady, linear fashion. Women's employment advanced more easily in new jobs or services where there was no long history of exclusive male employment. Thus, between 1900 and 1914, a period of particularly sharp growth in communication services, women's employment advanced most rapidly in a completely new employment field, in telephone services which had come under the aegis of the Postal Administration in 1889.[8]

In additition to challenging or deepening the historical basis of interpretations of women's work, a detailed study of this kind serves the important purpose of restoring human actors to the historical events, permitting us to witness how they participated in and experienced change. With hindsight one may indeed view the feminization of clerical work as an inevitable stage in the development of industrializing societies. But for employers, beset by fears and doubts, the decision to hire women was often an experiment that time and experience would or would not prove to be worth maintaining or extending. For critics, often upset by women's initial appearance in a man's world, nothing seemed inevitable or even irreversible.

Most importantly, the women workers become visible. The first generations of postal employees were pioneers as much as the more glamorous first women lawyers or first women professors, whose dates of entry into the professions during this same period figure so much more prominently in the historical record. If the identity of much more ordinary wage-earners like the postal workers has often been lost to history, is it not partly owing to historians' own inability to escape the usual identification of women workers with the denigrating abstraction "cheap labor"? Although this study does offer one more indisputable example of women's relatively weak position in wage economies, most of the women whose stories will be told were anything but the weak, passive, dependent female creatures of the nineteenth-century stereotype. If their choices were limited by external conditions, they nonetheless sought both on their own and through collective organizations of employees to gain more autonomy in their work lives and greater financial well-being for themselves and their dependents. Their efforts are all the more admirable because their lives failed to conform to conventional expectations: generally having long, uninterrupted careers—itself a rarity for women in the period—the *postières* risked social disapproval whether they never married or whether they married and remained working after marriage. Thus while we know that the "untraditional" employment paths they first took were to become "traditional" ones for succeeding generations of women, this knowledge should temper only our evaluation of the long-term significance of the change, not our appreciation of the first *postières'* stores.

Chapter One:
The Feminization of
Provincial Postal Work

Long before female clerks ever appeared in urban post offices, women worked as managers of provincial bureaus in France. In her *Souvenirs d'une vieille Femme* (1861), Sophie Ulliac Trémadeure (1794-1862), a prolific novelist and journalist of the nineteenth century, left us an early portrait of the *directrice des postes*. During an official visit to Clermont-sur-Oise, a provincial bourg of 2,715 inhabitants, fifty-eight kilometers from Paris, Mlle Trémadeure found lodging overnight with a *directrice,* a widow and mother of two. The year was 1837 or thereabouts:

> I learned that evening how much work the management of a post office required. While preparing her dispatches, tying them up and sealing them after having stamped each letter, Mme C*** described the thousand details that comprised her work day and night. The *courriers* certainly were not as numerous as they are today but the *directrice* was then obliged to leave her bureau at any hour and in all kinds of weather to go to open the mail trunk with the key she entrusted to no one, and take the dispatches addressed to her bureau. Today the dispatches are kept in a pouch closed with a padlock to which the *directrice* has a key, and which each *courrier* carries right into the bureau.
>
> At midnight and the sound of a carriage pulling up, Madame C*** lit a bright lantern, took her dispatches, put on some heavy clogs, hastily threw a shawl over her head and ran to the door.
>
> The weather was dreadful outside; the rain mixed with snow fell in torrents, swept about by a strong wind. I had followed Madame C***, but I stopped at the threshold of the door. From there I admired the equanimity with which she performed her

duty and obligingly answered the questions posed by the *courrier* who was perched on his gig over the mail trunk. The passengers inside the closed carriage had opened the door window a crack to a survey curiously this scene. Returning to the house, Mme C*** removed her dripping wet shawl and opened the pack of dispatches. She put each one into a particular slot in the large set of pigeon-holes, then she undid the package addressed to Clermont and stamped all the letters. In the interval that had passed between the arrival of the two *courriers,* she had changed the date on all the postmarks, . . . switching that day to the next.

Now, she says, we can go to sleep; two other *courriers* will pass between 4 and 5 o'clock this morning, but my sister will be the one to take them and distribute the letters and journals to the mail carriers.[1]

In the nineteenth century the *directrice des postes* became a personnage of folkloric dimension across the picturesque provincial landscapes. As with all features of those landscapes, many details escaped the view of even the most perceptive passer-by or local inhabitant. Who were these *directrices des postes?* How had the management of provincial post offices become women's work? The answers to these questions will help us understand how, by the late nineteenth century, some commentators would come to regard women's employment in provincial services as a precedent worthy of imitation in the cities, while others were to use the same example to oppose the introduction of women into urban locales.

Under the Old Régime the *poste* employed women. Royal archives show that of the roughly 1,000 municipalities of sufficient administrative and commercial importance to have their own post office, about one of five had a woman manager at some point in the eighteenth century.[2] During this era, when the reading and writing public was small and the bulk of mail related to matters of state, the work of most post office managers offered only part-time employment. In most locales the post office adjoined or was simply one corner of the official's dwelling. The commercial character and domestic setting of provincial postal services worked to keep the positions in the same family. Moreover, in the seventeenth century, management of a post office had been a venal office bought from the king; even after this practice had ended, the state continued to conform to the tradition "of the right of inheritance" in making appointments.[3] Correspondingly, the "property" holders were, regardless of sex, of bourgeois or aristocratic origins.

Owing to the pattern of family succession, women could be found managing post offices in major cities on the order of importance of Toulouse, Marseille, or Strasbourg. The only notable cities which did not have *directrices* as managers of the national mail service in the eighteenth century were Paris, Lyon, Bordeaux, and Rouen.[4] Women also ran local mail services controlled by the privately owned *Petite Poste* in Paris. The *Almanach Royal* for 1789 shows *directrices* in five of eleven neighborhood bureaus. In both positions, as manager of major provincial post offices and in the *Petite Poste* in Paris, women had the responsibility of overseeing the work of male clerks as well as the mail carriers who were also usually men.[5] In these situations, women's authority over men was based on their higher social origins as well as their marital status: most *directrices des postes* under the Old Régime were widows or wives who had succeeded to the positions held by their husbands until the latters' death, retirement, or resignation. It was much less common for an unmarried daughter to succeed her mother or father, and if she did so it was usually in a post office of lesser importance.[6]

The history of one family illustrates the particular role women played as widows, wives, and mothers in successive generations of postal employees. In 1760 Raymond Filiol de Raimond, a barrister of noble origins, became *directeur des postes* at Besançon (Doubs). Upon his death in 1774 he was replaced by his widow, Louise-Adélaïd Poulain du Clos, the daughter of an army captain. That same year the Widow Raimond promised to obtain the position for her son as a stipulation in his marriage contract:

> The said mother of the betrothed monsieur agrees to house, feed, heat and light the monsieur and demoiselle, future spouses, their children . . . and their servants, until the said Madame de Raimond obtains for the said monsieur, her son, the management of posts at Besançon.[7]

The widow did not delay in obtaining her son's appointment in her stead. In 1775 Louis Filiol de Raimond, also a barrister by training, became *directeur* at Besançon, and his mother retired to a Benedictine convent where she lived until her death in 1788. Raimond was *directeur* at Besançon for fifteen years, until 1790, when he was named inspector of postal services for the Doubs. At that time his wife, Mélanie Suzanne Isnard, took over direction of postal services in Besançon. Under normal circumstances she would have remained *directrice* until one of her two sons was old enough to assume the position. This possibility was cut short by the Revolution. In 1792 post office managers became elected officials, and Madame Raimond failed to be elected because of the aristocratic origins of her husband.[8]

As the history of the Besançon post office suggests, men also became post office managers by succeeding relatives. They were usually the sons of fathers who had died or retired or mothers who had held the position until sons came of age or married. Occasionally a man became *directeur des postes* after marrying a *directrice* who subsequently resigned in her husband's favor. The length of employment for men was, therefore, generally longer than for women. Other postal positions, from clerk through inspector and higher ranks, were more detached from principles of heredity, from a domestic setting, and from succession patterns associated with provincial post offices. Men alone filled all these positions. Career men typically entered employment between the ages of sixteen and twenty-five, after having finished their secondary studies or having served an apprenticeship in the office of a magistrate or notary.[9]

Most Old Régime patterns of recruitment survived the Revolution. It is true that in one petition to the National Assembly in the year II (1792-1793), a group of mail carriers urged that women be "retired" from all post offices:

> . . . Do away with women employees appointed *Directrices* and give them a pension. Is it suitable for women to manage . . . a bureau in which the man, who knows his merit and his rights, has to submit to the yoke of caprice, while he knows that the woman in physical terms does not possess but half his strength?[10]

Their wishes went unheeded, however. Even the revolutionary practice of election and the denial of women's suffrage did not preclude the election of women. A list of "reelected postal *directeurs* with thirty or more years of service" shows four women among the forty-seven *directeurs* who had escaped the ravages of disease, old age, or revolutionary purges.[11] In any case, the system of election was short-lived, and women continued after the revolution to be appointed provincial *directrices des postes* by succeeding other family members.[12]

There was one significant change. In the early nineteenth century the *directeurs* of post offices in the most important departmental capitals *(préfectures)* and commercial centers were without exception men. Nor could women any longer be seen managing post offices in Paris.[13] Gradually women were to disappear from all post offices important enough to have at least one salaried clerk who assisted the *directeur*. Thus in 1806 women ran twenty-four of these so-called *bureaus composés* (then totalling 181), including bureaus in La Rochelle, Nancy, Dunkerque, and Versailles; by 1834 there were but two *directrices* in *bureaux composés,* in La Rochelle and Clermont-Ferrand. Exceptions were no longer made even for widows, who in the period 1806 to 1834 had filled most of the positions in *bureaux composés.*[14]

In return, the development of postal services began to favor an increase in women's employment in lesser locales, such as the post office at Clermont-sur-Oise. Between 1835 and 1850, the number of provincial post offices, hitherto stable, almost doubled, from 1,443 to 2,679, most of the increase due to the opening of bureaus in municipalities formerly without services.[15] The institution of a daily mail service in all post offices beginning in 1827, and the creation of a rural delivery service in 1830, aided the growth of mail volume. In accordance with the increasing importance of the communication services for commercial growth, the Postal Administration passed conflict of interest rules, which made it difficult for *directeurs* to combine their postal duties, as they had frequently in the past, with other positions such as shopkeeper or notary.[16] As a consequence, the management of old and new post offices in lesser locales began to fall to women by default. By 1841 women managed 61 percent (953 of 1,563) of the *"bureaux à taxation,"* so called because the manager's salary depended on the amount of postal taxes taken in. Though sometimes higher, salaries in these positions ranged typically from 400 to 1500 francs annually, compared to the fixed salaries of 2200 to 3200 francs earned by managers of *bureaux composés.*[17] Women outnumbered men earliest as managers of the *bureaux à taxation* in the more developed, mostly northern regions of France, where alternative employment opportunities for educated men, including those in the Postal Administration, were more numerous.[18]

Unwritten traditions and *ad hoc* rulings set the boundaries of woman's place in the Postal Administration, but in 1844 an ordinance formally spelled out the conditions for women's employment as *directrices des postes*. First, in reserving appointments for women related to someone who had served the state in a civil or military capacity, the law codified prevalent attitudes and practices which viewed women's appointments as a means of compensating their families, and, thereby, helping solidify families' devotion to the state.[19] A second stipulation of the 1844 ordinance restricted women's initial appointment to post offices yielding incomes of 1000 francs or less. Once appointed, *directrices* had the right to "hierarchical advancement," but "women could in no instance," the law read, "be called to manage *bureaux composés*."[20] Soon after women were also excluded from any kind of post office located in the seat of a *sous-préfecture*, an administrative subdivision, or in any city with a Magistrate's or commercial court.[21]

Postal yearbooks indicate that, in practice, women's employment conformed closely to the law. From 1860 well into the twentieth century, no women managed *bureaux composés*, which were found in all department *préfectures* and commercial centers. Moreover, the proportion of female managers in *sous-préfectures* dropped from 53 percent to 12 percent between 1842 and 1860, and by 1880 no women managed bureaus in these lesser administrative centers.[22]

As Julie Daubié first pointed out in 1866 in her long essay demanding women's equal access to all occupations and professions, the regression of women from management of more important post offices reflected "administrative centralization," or the increasing role of the state in regulating postal appointments at the expense of the family.[23] If women were losers in the process, the explanation lies in great part beyond the postal service itself, in woman's place in the wider French economy, society, family, and law. Daubié understandably looked back on the late eighteenth and early nineteenth centuries as a kind of golden age of postal work, when the two sexes were "on a perfectly equal footing." Recalling that at one time women proved themselves to be and were considered as fit as men to run post offices in major cities was important; this fact had escaped most everyone by the late ninteenth century. But Daubié was incorrect in her estimate of equality in the earlier period: women had never been on a wholly equal footing with men. Family ties were more important in explaining the specific roles of women in the early postal service.

An immediate contributing factor in the exclusion of women from post offices yielding the highest salaries was the campaign waged by postal clerks and their supporters in *La France Administrative,* a journal edited in the early 1840s by clerks in central ministries in Paris. In the five years of *La France Administrative's* appearance, scarcely an issue passed without some reference to women's employment as *directrice des postes.* Threatened by the numerical predominance of women, one writer asserted that "the administration was falling under the dominance of the distaff," while another called women "the greatest plague of the postal administration."[24] When contributors focused on women's management of post offices in administrative centers, they made statements to the effect that "a man always represents the postal administration with greater dignity in important locales where there reside numerous functionaries with whom the *directeur* had daily business dealings."[25] Though generally sympathetic toward the employment of widows or single women without dowries, editors cast slurs on all *directrices* when they wrote of women's indiscretion and recounted stories of the "scandalous conduct of certain *directrices*" who left their post offices to domestic servants while they "gallavanted about."[26] Nourishing such hostile feelings were the grievances of men clerks against the administration. Particularly problematic was their lack of promotional opportunities, which they hoped would increase if they instead of women were appointed managers of certain post offices. *La France Administrative's* charges also reflected actual instances of abusive favoritism, where men or women obtained relatively handsome appointments through political connections.[27]

One feminist journal of the day took up the defense of women in the *poste,* although it failed to have an impact on policy. *La Gazette des Femmes* (1836-1868) was an organ of well-to-do feminists who demanded political and civil rights for women, the development of girls' education, and the equal access of women to careers in the professions, business, and civil service. In a front page editorial in 1841, Louise Riberolles described as "reactionary and absurd" any notion that women were indiscreet, morally lax, or in other ways less fit than men to be *directeurs des postes.* She added that women were particularly well suited for the job which demanded only "order, regularity, and a continual supervision."[28]

The dual process of the feminization of provincial postal work and the exclusion of women from the management of urban post offices served a crucial function. As the Director of Posts would later state in a different but analogous context, "competition by many low-level employees for a much smaller number of advanced positions made the good employees suffer at the expense of the mediocre, harmed morale, affected efforts to ensure the continued recruitment of personnel, and in general, hindered the smooth-running of services.''[29] The segregation of women and men, first, into different entry-level jobs, women as *directrices* of secondary post offices and men as clerks, and, second, on distinctive career ladders, was the earliest hierarchical division of the white-collar work force which alleviated competition between the sexes for advanced positions. Whether or not male clerks appreciated it, the fact that women continued to capture most appointments as managers of lesser bureaus helped their own future prospects. With few men entering the Postal Administration at this position there were fewer male employees over all who could aspire for promotion to higher grades which were reserved for men.

The number of secondary bureaus continued to proliferate after 1850. Mail volume expanded dramatically after 1848, when the legislature introduced the first postal stamps and lowered and unified postal rates, doing away with the awkward system of taxation by distance. The steady development of railroad transportation resulted in the rapid demise of mail transport by horse and carriage over long distances. Mail delivery was further speeded after the introduction of ''ambulatory'' postal wagons, which carried clerks sorting mail along rail routes between cities. The development of postal services reflected, and in turn aided, wider commercial growth and the reduction of illiteracy.

By 1880, over 4,000 women were dispersed throughout provincial France, running four-fifths of all post offices where the manager worked unassisted by a salaried clerk.[30] While women had run only a small fraction of post offices in this category in the early nineteenth century, management of these *"bureaux simples"* had come to appear almost by nature as ''women's work.'' Describing the low salaries and dead-end character of the employment in the *Dictionnaire des Professions* (1880), Edouard Charton asserted that the work was suitable only for women who might find in the employment an ''honorable situation.'' Similarly, in the *Dictionnaire de l'administration française* (1878), Maurice Block classified the position under the rubric' ''women.''[31] In the meantime, most people had forgotten that women had at one time managed neighborhood post offices in Paris and main bureaus in cities like Toulouse and Marseille.

The hundreds of women who worked as *directrices des postes,* or rather as *receveuses des postes,* as they were called after 1864, seemed equally unaware of how the character of women's employment in the post had altered over time. Instead, upon receiving her appointment papers, many a successful applicant must have agreed with the opinion expressed by one writer that the reservation of lesser post offices for women showed an "enlightened, generous, kind, and paternal sollicitude." Other appointees must have joined their colleague, Clara Séverine Lériche, who vowed "to prove herself worthy through the care and attention" she brought to her new duties.[32] The need for a respectable livelihood overshadowed all other considerations.

Chapter Two:
Receveuses des Postes:
Women's Work in the Country

While "women" in the abstract had more rights in postal services under the Old Régime, more real women benefited from the increased opportunities for employment as *receveuse des postes.* Moreover, once the position of managing post offices was no longer regarded as a kind of inheritable family property and as the number of post offices grew, the work became accessible to women of more modest social origins. More and more exceptional were the employees of aristocratic origins portrayed in fiction from Sainte-Beuve's *Christel* to Elie Berthet's popular novel, *La Directrice des Postes* (1861). In these stories, the further the heroines had fallen in station by seeking employment, the more pitiable they seemed and the more romantic their eventual reversal of circumstances through newly found wealth and princely marriage suitors.

Still, compared to the typical female wage-earner in the nineteenth century, the women who became *receveuses des postes* constituted an elite. Usually the offspring of better-educated parents who comprised the middle strata of civil servants and military personnel, they were the products of an above-average education for women. By virtue of their education and origins, they neither set their vision toward a career, like their fathers or brothers, nor accepted the imperative of salaried work at the age of ten or eleven, as did many working-class French girls. Instead, they had been socialized to marry and to regard salaried employment as demeaning. Their education and upbringing were inextricably embedded in a web of middle-class ideals concerning woman's place and the real, limited employment opportunities for women of this class.

Force of circumstance compelled most women to seek employment as *receveuse des postes.* The Postal Administration was, as one writer put it, "a refuge for *déclassées.*"[1] Prefectural files on *receveuses* are filled with letters backing one applicant or another from sub-prefects, mayors, judges, legislative deputies, the applicants' relatives, and the women themselves, which attest to the applicants' economic straits. Even though applicants whose families had greater political leverage were most favored in the heavy competition, all women had to try to demonstrate financial need. The letters illustrate the particular character of many an applicant's need, namely, impoverishment owing to a change in the family's financial situation rather than outright poverty.

There was Mlle Bévenot, for example, whose father had been employed in the Weights and Measures Administration for twenty-three years when he died leaving a widow and three children "in a most precarious position." Demoiselle Bévenot's cousin pleaded for his relative's appointment, declaring that the income from postal employment combined with her older sister's income from teaching "would shelter the family from want." The applicant's file also included a letter from a high court officer who assured the prefect that the deceased civil servant's daughter was "worthy of interest."[2] Other applicants included the daughter of a university professor who died leaving eight children penniless; the daughter of the mayor of Marchiennes (Nord) who was actively employed but had problems supporting his six children; the young widow of a prefectural employee in the Somme who had died during the cholera epidemic of 1866 leaving his wife the sole supporter of her mother, father, and ten-month old child; a retired army captain's daughter who wrote: "Misfortune strikes me in the very person of my husband who has abandoned me, leaving me a young child without any means of support."[3] One applicant, Eugénie Longueval, was supported in her candidacy by a petition from the governing body of the municipality of Rosendaël (Nord), where there was a vacancy to be filled. The petition went:

. . . from a wealthy family, struck by ill fortune, the mother of Mlle Longueval has been reduced to a most critical state, and it is her daughter, Eugénie, sacrificing the small inheritance she had counted on for her future, who has obtained for her mother that which her age and her former situation render necessary.
      In these circumstances . . . and stressing to you again that Mlle Longueval's family holds a justly honored position in your region, the undersigned believe [Mlle Longueval worthy of your interest] . . .

Several members of the Longueval family have been
mayors and adjoints in Loon over a period of many years and
the present Adjoint, M . . . . , is [the applicant's] first
cousin . . . . [4]

Though fewer in number than under the Old Régime, the female
relatives—widows and daughters—of postal employees continued
throughout the nineteenth century to fill a large proportion of postal
appointments. Relatives of postal employees were most familiar
with the possibility for employment as *receveuse,* and were also
often already well-acquainted with their duties even before receiving formal appointments. The story of Irma Roland offers one example of the postal family. Irma was the daughter of Françoise
Roland, *receveuse des postes* at Falaise (Calvados). Irma's father,
also a postal employee, had died when she was young. The widow
Roland provided for Irma and her sister, Pauline, as best she could,
with income from her work and a small inheritance. Through her
mother's efforts and will, Irma had received an extended schooling,
first in a boarding school, then with male tutors in her home—an ap-
propriate education for a girl who, in the world of Falaise, was "someone, Mademoiselle Roland, the daughter of the *[receveuse] des
postes.*" In ensuring her daughters' education, perhaps Irma's
mother had foreseen the day when she would no longer be able to
provide for them. In the summer of 1832, the inheritance having
long dried up and unable to live on their mother's salary, the two
women, aged twenty-six and twenty-seven, were compelled to leave
home and "take their chances each one on her own." Following in
her mother's footsteps, Irma sought appointment as *receveuse,*
while her sister became a private schoolteacher.[5]

MARITAL STATUS AND POSTAL EMPLOYMENT

The trend toward the appointment of single, dowryless women
was established by the 1840s, and in the last quarter of the century,
three out of four new appointees were single and most of the rest
were younger widows.[6] As early as the Revolution, feelings of pity
toward the single woman without a dowry had found public expression alongside mail carriers' protests over women managers. In a
petition addressed to the National Assembly in 1789, one
anonymous citizen had written:

Would it not be just to reserve for women all kinds of bureaus . . . and whatever positions might be at hand? You cannot envisage with indifference the numerous unfortunate girls who are unable to buy themselves a spouse. Forsaken . . . when they lost their parents, they vegetate in indigence and tears, grumbling against the injustice of their lot . . . . [7]

It was in the same paternalistic spirit that Napoleon I had established the Legion of Honor boarding schools for the impoverished daughters of legionnaires, excellent institutions located at St. Denis and Ecouen which were to send many a graduate into the Postal Administration.[8] In addition to solicitude for single women, other factors promoting the greater proportion of unmarried women among new appointees included the declining importance of family ties in appointments, the proliferation of new post offices, and the institution, in 1853, of guaranteed pensions for all civil servants, which upon men's deaths, fell to their widows.

Rather than renouncing marriage in seeking postal employment, many women regarded the position as their last resort in trying to fulfill this goal. In one letter written regarding a Madame Roethel, her husband, a schoolteacher, explained in passing that his wife "had brought [him] her position as a dowry."[9] Indeed the rapidity with which marriage usually followed appointment suggests that the position often represented a dowry: of women appointed near the end of the century, almost a third (29 percent) of those who married did so within two years of their appointment, nearly half (49 percent), within four years. Such speed reflected the relatively advanced age at which women began employment as well. Half of all single women were over twenty-seven and only a small fraction had succeeded in obtaining a special dispensation to the rule setting the minimum age at twenty-five. As a consequence, women who did marry tended to do so at a relatively old age. While the average age at first marriage was twenty-four for Frenchwomen in the last quarter of the century, the average age of women post office managers was thirty-three, two out of three marrying at thirty or older.

Marriage rates remained low, however, as over half of all women who became *receveuses* at the end of the century never married. The care of aged parents or younger siblings and relatives was a factor hindering marriage. Another was the problem of insufficient resources to attract a husband of similar educational background and social standing, which was aggravated by employment in isolated provincial locales and conflict of interest rules which prohibited marriage with tradesmen. The result of social convention and employment conditions was that many women were fated to remain "old maids," as one writer remarked, "unless these ladies . . . consent to marry carpenters or masons."[10] Scattered evidence for the occupations of *receveuses'* husbands confirms that suitable matches in marriage typically meant alliances with retired or still active civil servants, other white-collar employees, or property owners.[11]

As a result of the high proportion of single women among appointees and the low rate of marriage, 58 percent of all women post office managers in 1880 were either single women still hoping to marry or confirmed spinsters, compared to just 41 percent in 1850.[12] This meant that many women were the chief or only breadwinners in their households: for example, in 63 percent (forty-two of sixty-six) of *receveuses'* households in the department of the Seine outside Paris, and in 62 percent (eighteen of twenty-nine) in the Mediterranean department of the Hérault.[13] The continuing need of married and single women alike to work for a living produced a very low turnover rate. Most *receveuses* were to have long, uninterrupted careers.[14]

THE RELATIVE ATTRACTIONS OF POSTAL EMPLOYMENT

Whether or not marriage eventually followed appointment, every new appointee's immediate concern was to earn a livelihood which put her education to use. As one woman wrote, her appointment permitted her "to reap the fruits of the relatively good education that father had provided at the price of real sacrifices."[15] In view of the privileged educations most *receveuses* had received in boarding schools or other kinds of private institutions, the written aptitude examination required for admission to postal employment had been the least of their hurdles.[16] If their letters found in prefectural archives are representative, there is no doubt that the women comprised a highly literate group of employees. Even before perusal of the texts for substantive details, the reader is struck at first glance by the form: the clearly written, carefully formed words, the well-structured sentences and paragraphs, the absence of grammatical or spelling mistakes.

In the work of *receveuse,* women used their reading, writing, and computational skills to perform a variety of clerical tasks. These included certifying receipt of the mails, sorting letters, journals, and circulars, weighing and calculating postal rates for letters and packages, and keeping daily and monthly accounts. The supervision of the work of the two or three mail carriers who worked out of most lesser post offices required skills similar to those used in the management of household servants. As one manual advised, the *receveuse* was assured of "keeping the mail carriers within the strict limits of their duties" if she avoided "all familiarity with them, restrained from asking them to assist her with personal chores, kept her opinions of each mail carrier to herself, and was fair under all circumstances." And she was urged to maintain toward all her mail carriers equally, "a reserve embued with dignity, the latter assuring her of the respect and esteem of her subordinates."[17] Similarly, the emphasis given in their upbringings to gentility and good manners helped the *receveuses* in their contacts with other civil servants and the public in an age when urbanity was still a highly valued and expected feature of the civil servant's comportment. The women's backgrounds were also additional insurance (supplementing the required security deposit against financial losses) that the state was, as one commentator put it, "better served and with the greatest loyalty and in the best conditions of morality."[18]

As civil servants, *receveuses* escaped the manual jobs which provided employment for most women in the nineteenth century as well as the seasonal unemployment associated with such work. They had complete job security: gross neglect of duties, outright abandonment of functions or embezzlement of funds were about the only circumstances to produce dismissal, and even in such instances, the Administration was often benevolent in pardoning and readmitting offenders.[19] The triumph of republicanism in the 1870s apparently did not threaten this security. There is no evidence that any women were removed from office for political reasons.

Further, in many regions of France the *receveuse des postes* was "someone." The word "Administration" represented something formidable, and the civil servant basked in its considerable prestige. In the memoirs of one *receveuse, Au Service du Public durant quarante ans* (1929), Mme S. de Lange captured this mentality well:

> Thus I arrived . . . at T . . . surrounded by a halo . . . .
> During my term there I did nothing that could diminish the
> high opinion that the people had of me . . . .

I rendered all kinds of services. We [she and her husband] filled the role of private secretary for many persons who were unsure of themselves . . . What gratitude! Baskets of vegetables, fruits, old bottles [of wine] with stories behind them, invitations to family celebrations . . . . [20]

Finally, moralists often pointed to another commendable feature of the work that had helped establish the tradition of women's work as provincial post office manager; namely, employment in a domestic setting.[21] The ability to tend to household, children, or other family members—aged parents, for example—was important in an era when post offices were open long hours—ten hours a day, seven days a week—but when the work itself was seldom intensive. As exceptional as these women civil servants were in the nineteenth century, their work conflicted minimally with household responsibilities and, correspondingly, with cultural attitudes which viewed women's primary sphere as the family and home.

An excerpt from an early literary caricature entitled "The *Directrice Pot-au-Feu*" indicates the domestic character and social approval of this work:

. . . With one hand they stir the kettle, with the other apply the stamp.

They send off their mail carrier for the daily round, and at the same time, their servant for the marketing.

They figure the bill for the laundry and the dairy at once with the end of the month's accounting sheet.

The same string they use to lace their chicken serves to tie their packages of dispatches.

. . . But next to that, everything runs smoothly and the *directrice pot-au-feu* is easily the best woman around and the most accomodating postal employee there is. She opens her bureau in the morning at the first song of her bullfinch and does not close it in the evening until after the last mouthful of salad at supper. All this to the grand satisfaction of the voyager delayed either *en route* or at the pub.

. . . Touching merger of the *Directrice* and the housekeeper lending each other a hand to shape an entirely fine person.[22]

Considering this portrait and other expressions of the same sentiment, one can easily imagine the objections that would be raised when women were first introduced into urban workplaces and the real problems that women who worked outside the home would face.

ANOTHER VIEW OF WOMEN'S WORK IN THE COUNTRY

In reality, of course, certain aspects of the *receveuse*'s work undermined the idealized domestic tranquility, as has already been suggested by the high number of women who never married despite the ability to work in the home. Sophie Ulliac-Trémadeure's description of the manager greeting the *courrier* at odd hours of the night captures one of the most disagreeable aspects of the post office manager's routine. Because of this task and the early opening and late closing of the post office, the *receveuse*'s freedom of movement was in general very restricted. The lodging with adjoining office became most confining for the women who lived alone and therefore had no one to spell them from their official duties. The same women suffered most from social isolation in the locales with the least business and lowest salaries to which most new appointees were assigned. According to one journalist's description, first assignment was typically to a "miserable village where life was dull, without distraction, without movement: the rural mail carrier each morning, the gendarme once or twice a week, the curé or rector from time to time—that is all."[23] In these circumstances, it is not surprising that in a report dated 1880, one official termed "retiring" the life-style of most women who ran post offices in his department.[24]

Such a characterization also suggests that few women merited the popular folklorish image portraying the *receveuse* as gossipy and indiscreet. Rather, the portrait reflected the mentality of the small community, which closely scrutinized the conduct of any outsider in its midst. Though most women were appointed to their regions of origin, only in rare instances did someone have the good fortune to fill an opening in her hometown. In their eagerness to win appointment, most (but not all) women had accepted any residence: as one *receveuse* had written, she "was indifferent regarding the locale as long as [she was] promptly appointed."[25] With isolated locations often went cramped and insalubrious lodging, but if this provided another reason for some women to refuse certain residences, the consideration was also necessarily secondary for women pressed to have employment. Thus, having found the lodging "a little small," one *receveuse* tried to look on the brighter side, at the "quite large garden" and "healthy countryside."[26]

Once installed, the *receveuse*, as the entrusted guardian of the citizens' mail, had to strive to maintain the public's confidence and respect. This task, more difficult in certain regions than others, required diligence, patience, tact, and deference—all the good breeding a woman could summon to her public contacts. If the *receveuse* failed to show good humor in the face of the public's demands, she earned no baskets of fruit and bottles of wine, but rather a reputation as "shrewish" and "cantankerous." In extreme cases of personality conflicts, the municipality registered a complaint, often trumping up the charges, to seek the *receveuse*'s transfer to another residence so that someone more compliant might replace her. *Receveuses* also sometimes found themselves in the middle of political struggles between local factions, even though as a group they were reputed to care little themselves about politics.[27] In either instance, the departmental director of postal services made the necessary inquiries, occasionally finding a *receveuse* guilty of indiscretion. In such cases, he punished the offender by sending her to another residence and sometimes reducing her salary as well. But more commonly, the director took the post office manager's side after judging the complaints exaggerated.[28]

Regardless of residence, few new *receveuses* escaped living on a tight budget. In rural communities where most families were self-sufficient and little integrated into the money economy, an important class marker was distance from the level of subsistence. The fact that the *receveuse* was often one of the few salaried employees in the community put a certain social distance between herself and others. Yet, before 1865 the typical, fixed salary of 600 francs provided just barely a living wage, and the same was true of the minimum wage of 800 francs annually which was set thereafter. One employee's itemized budget showed that in one year she spent 530 francs on food and 241 francs on other living expenses not fully covered by the administrative allotment for rent and costs of running the post office. Little remained for personal expenses such as clothing, which was also essential to maintaining social distinction.[29] Describing the dilemma, one woman wrote, "If the *receveuse* does not try to keep social rank out of self-pride—she who has generally received a good education and is used to certain comforts—she must do it for the administration she has the honor to represent."[30] "Keeping

FIGURE 1. Rural Post Office (c. 1900). The older woman on the left leaning out the window is probably the *receveuse*, the younger woman her assistant or daughter. (Courtesy of Musée de la Poste)

rank'' was at once most important and most difficult in those locales where, as S. de Lange wrote, the people were ''well-off, educated, the most modest son of a peasant having been sent away to school.'' There the public tended to regard all civil servants as ''simpletons, vegetating in an inferior situation.''[31]

With such low wages, earning an honest living was sometimes difficult. Alongside the exceptional heroines of the postal services cited for courage in rescuing cashboxes from fire or theft were the handful of women sacked or, worse, imprisoned because, upon inspection, postal funds came up short.[32] If some of these cases involved premeditated embezzlement for aggrandizement, others were the result of impoverishment. The story was told, for example, of Nathalie Rolland, the daughter of an army surgeon who had died after a sudden illness, leaving Nathalie and her mother with no means of support. Appointed in 1880 after a friend's intervention in her behalf, Mlle Rolland was scarcely settled in her bureau at 800 francs annual salary, when the people who had lodged her and her mother in Paris presented them with a bill of 600 francs for services rendered. Panicked, the young woman took the money out of the post office's cashbox. Expecting the arrival of the inspector, she then stole the money from the mails to cover the deficit. Caught and brought to trial, she received a two-year prison sentence.[33] Less dramatic but equally telling were the more numerous instances of *receveuses* who received temporary suspensions or reprimands because of small deficits. Managers were strictly forbidden ''to take any credit on cashbox funds or to mix up their own funds with those of the Treasury.''[34] The interdiction in itself suggests that some employees were tempted in a pinch to borrow from the funds with the idea of later returning the money.

It is true that salary raises provided women with greater financial well-being over time. Nevertheless, owing to the limitations imposed by law and regulation upon women's advancement, the distance between minimum and maximum salaries remained short. Retirement lists show that, of the women who retired between 1866 and 1875, after an average twenty-eight years' service, almost half (48 percent) had attained salaries of less than 1400 francs at retirement while only a small fraction (2 percent) retired at salaries higher than 1800 francs.[35] Most women still employed in the 1880s reached a dead end at 1400 francs. A typical example, Jeanne Longaygues received three raises between her appointment in 1873 and her last increase to 1400 francs in 1881, and then remained at that salary for the rest of the decade.[36] Altogether, 92 percent of all women employed in 1890 earned salaries in the range of 800 to 1400 francs, with roughly half of this group blocked at the salary of 1400 francs, the maximum for post offices in the lowest classes where most women worked.[37]

As a consequence, women frequently adopted the strategy of requesting a change in residence, either to try to improve their salary or at the least to work in a more desirable locale. Of women appointed to manage post offices in the last quarter of the century, less than one-fifth (16 percent) managed the same post office throughout their employment, while fully a third (32 percent) changed residences three times or more. One peripatetic *receveuse* moved nine times within fourteen years and worked in six different departments.[38] Women also sought changes of residence for family reasons, such as to be closer to parents or to husbands' place of employment, but very few women returned to their hometown. Many a *receveuse* tried to speed her promotion or change in residence with help from influential personnages.[39]

Obviously there were limits to such strategies, since there were simply too many women seeking promotions to a limited number of vacancies. Only a handful of especially well-placed *receveuses* managed to obtain appointments to bureaus where the managers earned fixed salaries of 1600 to 2200 francs, plus an important supplementary income derived from special allowances and a cut of all postal receipts. Yet, even those few places were begrudged them. Echoing the sentiments first expressed in *La France Administrative* forty years earlier, "a group of forty-three clerks" protested women's appointment to such bureaus in a letter sent to *Le Journal des Postes,* a periodical where clerks and *receveuses* alike had found a forum to express their grievances beginning in 1867. The clerks' letter, appearing in 1887, went:

> We wish our gracious colleagues all the well-being possible, but really, everything has its correct place. The clerks who seek these bureaus are all married, fathers of families, overburdened, for the most part, by other expenses . . .
>
> Most of the women managing bureaus in this category are pensioned Widows or Demoiselles exempt from concerns regarding the future of children. It is easy to see the difference in the two conditions.[40]

The long, eloquent response of one "demoiselle" showed that at least some women aspired to higher-paying positions demanding more responsibility and considered their long years at salaries lower than those earned by clerks as just entitlement to compete for such promotions. The *receveuse* expressed her obvious bitterness at having been shortshrifted in her education and dowry to the profit of her brothers and continued:

> . . . One more thing. Not only did you not begin with our derisory salaries, but you also advanced much more rapidly and attained much higher salaries.
>
> If you began with the prospect of obtaining higher positions, we began with that of attaining the second class bureaus. We all knew that there would not be enough of these positions for all . . . But if you were mistaken in your calculations or if circumstances have betrayed your hopes, do you think, in all justice, that we ought to be the ones sacrificed? Then do not plead against favoritism. Satisfying your ambitions would represent the most absolute and odious act of favoritism.
>
> You have children, you say? That is a gratification not given everyone, at the same time that it is insurance for the old age. Do you believe that it is more just to devote yourself more to your descendants than to your ancestors? I think not . . . Our respective situations have their thorns, but leave it to the Administration to take care to soften our pains to the extent possible. But given that we are all in the same family, and in case that this happy moment does not come, I propose an arrangement, dear colleagues.
>
> I would be content to be confined to third class bureaus, but under one condition, only one condition: that your children in the name of which you would disinherit us, be charged by personal contract to make up for the insufficient resources of our old age. That will be an advantage for us and a source of honor for you.[41]

The details of the *receveuses'* stories obviously differed. It seems clear, however, that few women had sought employment as a means of independence and that once employed, few earned more than simply a modest livelihood. Rather than any overt desire for freedom, it was the constraints under which these women lived which helped shape their strength and courage, attributes that often drew the admiration of their granddaughters and great-granddaughters, who found these women models of independence. Still, it also seems certain that more than one of these *déclassées* raised without career goals and initially grateful for their appointments, became frustrated by the lack of opportunity. These women found support for their aspirations among avowed feminists outside the administration. Like their precursors of the 1840s, they demanded promotions for *receveuses* by evoking the rights of women to equality rather than simply the vaguer notion of fairplay.[42]

When change came to break the traditional patterns of job segregation in the Postal Administration, however, it was of a different order than envisioned by feminists seeking to improve the situation of *receveuses*. And rather than feminist demands for equality, internal labor problems which postal administrators sought to resolve imposed the change. Leaving the countryside, then, we head into the cities to witness the introduction of women into major urban post offices, not as post office managers, but as clerks.

Chapter Three:
The Feminization of Urban Services

The rapid development of postal services in the late nineteenth century set the stage for women's appearance as post office clerks in the cities. The triumph of republicanism in the 1870s provided a congenial political climate for the emergence of modern postal services. Traditionally viewed simply as a means of exchanging correspondence and producing in the process, revenues for the state, the *poste* emerged as a handmaiden to commerce and industry. The government agency assumed new functions such as the collection of commercial bills (1879), subscription to newspapers through postal money orders (1879), parcel post (1881), and the National Savings Bank (1882). The most important innovation of all was the merger of postal and telegraph administrations in 1878; a year later an autonomous Postal and Telegraph Ministry was established, free from the immediate fiscal grip of the Finance Ministry. The merger permitted economies of scale at the central and local levels. These savings in turn helped recover the short-term losses which resulted from the lowering, also in 1878, of postal and telegraph rates. With these rate changes, postal and telegraph circulation rose sharply. The greatest spurt came in the years immediately following the merger: aided by the good economic climate, total postal circulation increased by 52 percent over the four short years, from 1877 to 1881 (compared to a 29 percent increase over the decade 1882-1892).[1]

The work force simultaneously burgeoned in both urban and rural postal services. In the cities, a rapid influx of new clerks was required to operate telegraph machines, wait on customers in post offices, sort and dispatch mail. Initially, the Administration largely met this need in the customary manner by recruiting men. Between 1878 and 1883 alone, 7,400 men were admitted to postal employment through the national examination. This figure surpassed the total number of men employed as clerks in postal and telegraph services combined on the eve of the merger.[2] The reaction of one veteran clerk to the invasion of new recruits is telling. Albert Cim had entered telegraph services under the Second Empire, an era, he tells us, when clerks dressed for special occasions in "royal blue tunic[s] bedecked with brass buttons." "After the merger," writes Cim in his memoirs, "I sought to retire from the 'active duty' of the [neighborhood bureau in Paris] to take refuge in administrative offices."[3] In the relative calm of the ministerial bureaus, Cim, like many of his privileged cohorts, found the time to write several novels and pursue other literary interests.[4]

"Active" or "outside" services were indeed a different story, particularly in the archetypical urban setting of Paris. "What does one see in the Paris service? An agglomeration of employees who are always hurried and breathless, working in a feverish state of perturbation as they wait on the impatient public."[5] So wrote the Director General of Postal Services more than a decade before the merger. Owing to the centralization of communication and railroad services in Paris, over one-third to two-fifths of all French postal clerks were concentrated in the capital in the nineteenth century, and in the 1880s their number swelled to between three and four thousand.[6] The size of the offices employing clerks varied. Just over 600 clerks and chief clerks worked in shifts in the very large scale setting of the main Hotel des Postes on the rue du Louvre and more than 500 men at the telegraph central on the rue de Grenelle.[7] But many clerks continued to work in relatively small offices. The number of neighborhood post offices in Paris grew from sixty-one in 1877 to ninety-three by 1890. In the smallest post offices as few as two or three clerks worked under the *receveur's* supervision and even the larger post offices seldom employed more than ten clerks at one shift. Working in equally small groups were the ambulatory clerks who sorted and dispatched mail in the railroad wagons which moved mail from Paris to the provinces and back again.[8]

Despite the doubling of the total number of clerks nationally with the merger and expansion of services, Adolphe Cochery, Minister of Postal and Telegraph Services (1877-1885), failed to establish specialization within the clerical work force. He chose not to proceed in the manner proposed by some observers, that is, to recruit two groups: clerks to perform the more diverse tasks associated with postal counter work and the operation of sophisticated telegraph machines like the Baudot, and a lesser category of secondary employees to perform the more repetitious, mechanical tasks, like sorting mail or running the simple Morse telegraph.

The failure to introduce such a division undoubtedly reflected the desire to maintain a certain standard in recruitment. This goal was inherent in a series of reforms Cochery helped institute, including a raise in the clerk's starting salaries (from 1200 to 1500 francs in 1881), more regular promotions, and new training courses for apprentice clerks.[9] Though the more literary and classical features of the entrance examination failed to survive the merger, the *concours* remained a two-day affair, and the thrust persisted of testing general education rather than any practical knowledge of postal and telegraph regulations and operations. Part of the candidate's score included points the departmental examining board awarded for bearing and dress.[10] Both before and after the merger only a small fraction of clerks had completed secondary studies, but most men had had some schooling beyond the primary level.[11] Given these recruitment standards, it is easy to see why the experiment using former mail carriers as sorters on a limited scale at the Hôtel des Postes failed to catch on in the 1880s.[12]

Cochery was satisfied that he had improved recruitment of clerks. The number of candidates had increased as had their aptitudes and their education. Ameliorations in "the administrative career," reported Cochery in 1884, had attracted "young men formerly held back by the less certain and less advantageous prospects."[13] An analysis of recruitment patterns based on employee records suggests that Cochery's reforms at least held back a deterioration in standards of recruitment which might have accompanied a sudden expansion of the work force. Comparing the cohort of clerks who entered in the late 1870s and early 1880s to earlier cohorts, one discerns little change in the distribution of clerks by geographic regions of origin. Men from the less industrialized, mostly southern departments of France continued to fill a disproportionate number of jobs; but this trend, which derived from the existence of a single wagescale in postal services for all France, did not sharpen in the period immediately following the merger.[14] Nor was recruitment marked by a significant proletarianization of the clerical work force in terms of the clerks' social backgrounds. Before the merger, most clerks came from a fairly homogeneous, small town milieu of modest civil servants, transportation employees, small shopkeepers and artisans, and independent peasant-proprietors. After the merger, recruitment under Cochery saw a relative decline in the number of men from more middle-class backgrounds, particularly of sons of civil servants. But, again, the over-all trend was not as clear-cut as one might have predicted.[15]

In addition to the desire to maintain recruitment standards, a reluctance to establish specialization also reflected the need for flexibility and the inter-changeability of employees in different tasks and offices. That large numbers of clerks continued to work in small post offices in Paris as well as the provinces heightened the desirability of having "generalists," clerks familiar with the range of postal and telegraph operations and capable of exercising responsibility, tact, and judgment. Moreover, clerks were highly mobile and seldom remained in the same work place or even city over the course of their careers. Clerks, who all took the same examination, were haphazardly assigned to their initial jobs, and very soon jockeyed to improve their position by seeking transfers to other services or post offices. This kind of mobility was particularly characteristic of Parisian clerks, four-fifths of whom were of provincial origins and often sought transfers back closer to their home regions. Military service also interrupted the careers of many clerks, who were not necessarily assigned to their former work place on their return.[16]

The two goals, to maintain standards of recruitment and to uphold flexibility in the employment of clerks, help at once explain the particular function women filled in urban services after the merger as well as the constraints limiting their employment. The first women recruited as urban employees were hired as telegraph operators. Their purpose was to shore up the personnel at the Parisian telegraph central in anticipation of the sharp upsurge in telegraph messages after the rate decreases. At first only a "timid experiment" with sixty-six women in 1877, women's employment produced such promising results that the administration subsequently extended it on a larger scale. Between 1877 and 1883, the number of women telegraph operators at the telegraph central rose to 464, so that women alone almost accounted for the doubling of the personnel at the central over this period.[17] Soon after the merger, women were also introduced into the telegraph centrals at the Paris stock exchange and in the cities of Marseille, Lille, Bordeaux, Toulouse, Lyon, and Nantes.[18]

In using women to expand its telegraph personnel, France had followed on the heels of the British example. French telegraph experts and administrators had attentively read reports concerning the experience with women in British centrals.[19] Echoing the earlier words of the British director of telegraph services, Mr. Scudamore, who had maintained that "the wages which will draw male

FIGURE 2. Idealized engraving of first female telegraph employees in Paris (c. 1877). (Courtesy of Musée de la Poste)

operators from but an inferior class of the community will draw female operators from a superior class,'' French minister Cochery reported in 1882 that ''the recruitment of women is carried out under conditions of education generally superior to that demanded of new clerks.''[20]

It was not unusual for women in this first generation of urban employees to possess a teaching diploma, which distinguished the better-educated woman in this period.[21] Since employment opportunities for better-educated women in Paris and the provinces were extremely limited, administrators had no problems finding educated women ''locally,'' in or close to the cities of employment. Most of the women employed in Paris in the late 1870s and 1880s were from Paris, the suburbs, or departments contiguous to the department of the Seine.[22] These women received much lower starting salaries than most men in the administration. Like *receveuses,* their annual salary was 800 francs until 1893, when it was raised to 1000 francs. Women were barred entirely from the higher paying ranks of chief clerk or above. Thus, at this time, women represented cheaper and more locally available employees than men. Equally important, their recruitment did not require lowering entrance requirements. On the contrary, the recruitment of women, just like the improved standards of recruitment for men, worked to slow the proletarianization of the work force.

Still, the advantages of women notwithstanding, the number of the so-called *dames employées* remained disproportionately low in the 1880s. Fifteen years after 1877 there were less than 2,000 *dames employées* in Paris and the provincial cities. About half of these women were employed in large, central telegraph bureaus, the rest in the new field of telephone work.[23] Contrary to what one may have predicted, women played a negligible role in the rapid expansion of the urban work force following the merger. No women were introduced into postal services proper, either in larger central post offices or smaller neighborhood bureaus. The failure to recruit significant numbers of women in the 1880s for urban postal work is even more striking in view of the long, satisfactory experience of women's employment as *receveuses* in country post offices. In this instance, it seems clear that the second imperative of recruitment, that is, the need to maintain a flexible, mobile clerical work force, restricted the expansion of women's employment.

Accompanying cultural prescriptions about woman's place helped buttress the status quo. Whether clerks who sorted mail worked in post offices or on moving railroad cars, they did so in an atmosphere "permeated by specks of flying dust and the smoke and odor of melting sealing wax" used to close the pouches formed for expedition.[24] On the railroad cars, clerks suffered variously from "heat, cold, and lack of air."[25] Clerks in both settings had to work at particularly odd hours, late in the evening and early in the morning, and ambulatory clerks often traveled overnight. Considering these working conditions, it is not surprising that the dirtiest and most physically demanding tasks of heavy sorting and dispatching would remain men's work until the war of 1914-1918, when the necessity of employing women would temporarily fly in the face of middle-class niceties governing woman's place. Employment on postal railroad cars has remained men's work to the present day.

In comparison, the work of the post office counter clerk *(guichetier)* was less physically demanding, and specific job tasks closely resembled those already performed by the *receveuse.* But in the absence of necessity, the need for the interchangeability of clerks in different settings and cultural attitudes inhibited women's access to this urban post office work. Women's employment in the 1880s was predicated on the existence or establishment of separate work rooms for the two sexes and the segregation of women from the anonymous urban public. At the Paris telegraph central, for example, the large groundfloor work room was called *la salle des dames,* and the second floor, *la salle des hommes.* The beginning and end of the two sexes' shifts were staggered to lessen contacts between men and women before and after work.[26] In contrast, women's work in city post offices was, in the euphemistic language of the day, a more "delicate" problem. In 1876 the International Postal Union, an organization representing postal administrations in some twenty European countries and the United States, had concluded in a special report on women's employment that "any immediate contact with the public mass" or in groups with men employees was "irreconcilable with the vocation of women." Britain was the only European country at the time using women as post office clerks.[27] In fact, the French director of personnel in the postal ministry visited London in 1887 to observe first-hand women's work as postal counter clerks and returned to report the British example was "most satisfactory." But the "drawbacks" to making the change in France remained "unavoidable."[28]

Postal administrators may have foreseen opposition from men employees. Not everyone had greeted the introduction of women into urban telegraph services with unqualified approval. More than one clerk must have shared the feelings of an indignant colleague who wrote in the postal journal, *La Revue des Postes:* "This apparent superiority of the ladies over their colleagues of the stronger sex is illusory. In effect, the teaching diploma implies the knowledge of certain subjects that are not of demonstrable usefulness in the operation of the apparatuses." Clerks also insisted they had a higher output than women.[29] When the administration tried to introduce women into night work in 1888 in the telegraph service, the newcomers' welcome was decidedly inhospitable. As the sixteen women left the telegraph central in Paris after their shift, they were the objects of "an ovation" from their male colleagues that was "completely devoid of gallantry." Then, insult was added to injury when the women pioneers received, during their chaperoned trip home on a postal omnibus, a boisterous greeting from a troupe of students in the Latin Quarter.[30] This kind of charivari helped reinforce moral strictures regarding woman's place. Not incidentally, keeping women out of night work also served men's material interests, for night shift employees, assigned on rotation, received supplementary wages. Requiring that men do night work was also a guarantee that male telegraphists were indispensable, and would never be totally replaced by women.

Yet, women's introduction into telegraph work was on the whole a smooth one. Men could hardly complain that women undercut their wages, particularly during the "golden age" of the late seventies and early eighties when clerks' salaries were raised in order to upgrade the standard of recruits. The absence of the words *feminise* and *feminisation* from administrative and press descriptions in the 1880s indicates the general character of and attitudes toward women's employment in this period. Recruited as the work force was expanding, and then slowly and in selected locales, the numerical progression of women in telegraph work resulted more from the creation of new jobs rather than women's substitution for men. This is clear in the telegraph service, for although a form of telegraph service, Chappe's aerian system, had existed since the late eighteenth century, electric telegraph services were relatively new, having been developed in the 1860s.[31] The new telephone services employed women almost exclusively from the beginning, except for night work.[32] The same pattern prevailed for the employment of women to do paper work in administrative services. Most female office workers, about three-fourths of the 545 administrative employees in Paris in 1891, worked in central offices of the Postal Savings Bank. This institution used women from the time of its establishment to perform routine tasks of filing, verification, and copying.[33] With no precedence of ever having used women, which had aided, for example, the feminization of rural post office management, the recruitment of women as urban post office clerks would require more than simply the rapid expansion of urban services and the need for cheap, educated labor.

THE MERGER AND WOMEN'S WORK IN THE COUNTRY

In contrast to the limited employment of women in the cities, a growing number of women worked in secondary provincial post offices. It is important to return briefly to this arena to see how changes after the merger came to bear, in an unexpected way, on administrators' decision to place women in urban post offices in the early 1890s. The union of local postal and telegraph services under one roof had begun as early as 1873, so that almost two-thirds of all *receveuses* had responsibilities for both services by 1884. The establishment of new postal and telegraph offices in areas formerly without services provided additional jobs for women; by 1892 there would be over 5,300 *receveuses,* most of them managing combined postal and telegraph services.[34] More significantly, hundreds of young women, called *aides,* were needed to help the *receveuses* (and occasionally, *receveurs)* because of the addition of the telegraph and other new commercial and banking services. By 1880 there were already about 1,000 *aides,* and by 1892, an estimated 4,000.[35]

The growing complexity of services and the ensuing widespread use of *aides* produced a major change in the recruitment of *receveuses.* The increase in the number of tasks required of *receveuses* imposed the need for an apprenticeship period; in 1882 the administration made a one-year apprenticeship as *aide* a requirement for all candidates to the *receveuse* position. It also became essential that *aides* be given priority in appointments, since the principal motivation of women in becoming *aides* at very modest pay or none at all was to obtain eventual appointment as a full-fledged civil servant. If *aides'* aspirations were not fulfilled, their recruitment in turn would become difficult, and the execution of services in certain bureaus would become "impossible," forcing the hiring of regular civil servants at "enormous expense" to the budget. To ensure the fulfillment of its needs, the Postal Ministry all but wrested the prerogative of appointing *receveuses* from the departmental prefects, not all of whom gave up this power without minor battles.[36]

This democratization of recruitment, from exigency rather than principle, opened the door of postal employment to women of more heterogeneous social origins. Many daughters of civil servants continued to win appointments, but by the late 1880s these were almost always the daughters of modest, small-town civil servants (such as *receveurs* and *receveuses*, public schoolteachers, gendarmes, tax collectors).[37] Alongside these women and in even greater numbers were the daughters of the rural working and popular classes, many of whom had only a public school education.[38] This social promotion in many instances required considerable tenacity. The daughter of a deceased mail carrier, Marie Désirée Léonard, for example, had studied postal operations while continuing her miserably paid employment as private teacher, then worked another year and a half as *aide* with financial support from her family before being appointed *receveuse*.[39] The uphill climb was even tougher for *aides* of non-civil servant families, as they had to work for at least three years to win "personal title" to an appointment as *receveuse*. More generally, appointment presented an elusive goal as the number of *aides* burgeoned at a much faster rate than did openings as *receveuse*. In the 1880s, the administration made only about 150 to 200 appointments nationally each year, and competition was formidable: a spokesman estimated in 1885 that there were 100 candidates for every fifteen vacancies—ample justification for failing to hike *receveuses'* low starting salaries.[40] The introduction in the late 1880s of a system of ranking candidates by points—greatly diminishing the residual importance of political pull—reflected the critically intense competition for appointment.[41]

The opportunity for women to work in provincial post offices as *receveuses,* then *aides,* may in itself have helped perpetuate the traditional occupational segregation of the sexes: women in the country, men in the city. At the same time, however, the changes in postal services after the merger and, importantly, the *aide* system, contained the germ of this traditional segregation's demise. The distinction between post office managers who worked with salaried help and those who worked without began to break down. In some locales, such as the Paris suburbs, the *aide* was a full-time salaried employee in all but name and rights.[42] Moreover, the problem of having too many *aides* per civil service appointment continued to preoccupy administrators. They would not need a great leap of the imagination to think of using *"aides"* transformed into *"dames employées"* in urban post offices, particularly since the difference between the work of the *aide* and of the *dame employée* would be one of degree rather than kind.

THE FEMINIZATION OF URBAN POST OFFICES

The timing of the first experiment with women post office clerks—Paris in 1892—resulted from the conjuncture of several factors which together carried enough force and urgency to override the weight of bureaucratic inertia, social attitudes about woman's place, and over a hundred years of exclusive male employment. The onset in 1882 of what proved to be a long, drawn-out commercial crisis had a critical effect on postal services and the recruitment of men and women in country and city. The deterioration of the economic climate produced a budgetary crisis and the urgent need to economize. Reflecting the commercial crisis, total postal circulation grew relatively slowly after 1882 and in some years (1882 and 1886) actually fell. State revenues as a whole suffered, and between 1882 and 1887 the state faced its first budgetary deficits. The Finance Ministry and legislators in turn put a tightening clamp on the postal budget.[43]

In the cities, the relatively high standards of recruitment and employment conditions set in the halcyon days following the merger fell. As the bulging cohort of men clerks recruited in the late 1870s and early 1880s advanced in their careers to the point of achieving a modicum of financial security, promotions and raises suddenly evaporated. The "advancement crisis" of the late 1880s saw clerks blocked in their careers at the same civil service grade for four years, five years, and more. The interval between raises (of 300 francs) rose on average from 2 years, 3 months in 1883 to 4 years, 11 months by 1890. "Clerks" were shut out of "chief clerk" ranks to which formerly they had been almost automatically promoted.[44] Faced with the double problem of career blockages and budgetary cutbacks, Cochery's successors recruited fewer than a total of 1,000 men through the competitive examination in the seven years from 1884 to 1890. Ironically, the number of men who took the examination in this period was higher, as a result of the economic crisis, than any time since the merger.[45] Instead of "clerks," the administration relied almost exclusively on the recruitment of "auxiliary clerks" who were paid less (800-1000 francs) and who lowered the number of "clerks" competing for promotions. As a result, most men who became clerks in the late 1880s were younger than men recruited in the early years of the decade: on average, sixteen or seventeen rather than eighteen or nineteen and older. Moreover, these auxiliary clerks generally came from poorer backgrounds.[46]

In the short term, however, the system of using auxiliary clerks failed to improve existing clerks' situations. The latter's frustrations manifested themselves in the wave of collective protests—public assemblies, petitions, and work stoppages—that swept the work force, particularly in Paris, in the years 1887 to 1893.[47] Further, the system of recruiting auxiliaries itself proved untenable. When the auxiliary clerks' own expectations of winning appointment as regular clerks were frustrated, they protested, too, and won the sympathy of some more socially progressive legislators. Other legislators objected to the fall in standards signaled by the new system of recruitment. An amendment providing for the abolition of the auxiliary clerk grade narrowly failed in 1891, but after the 1892 elections, the new Chamber approved the measure.[48] In 1893 almost 1,000 auxiliary clerks became full-fledged clerks through the competitive examination, and by 1898 all auxiliaries had achieved full clerk status.[49] Yet, even before the formal suppression of the auxiliary clerk grade, its low salaries combined with poor prospects had produced recruitment difficulties in many northern departments.[50] This is not surprising considering that the auxiliary clerk's starting salary was equivalent to less than three francs daily in 1891, or less than half the average daily wage of 6.15 francs that male industrial workers in Paris received at this time.

From the postal administrators' point of view, clerks' protests and particularly the auxiliary clerks' victory, left them with an unchanged if not worse dilemma. Given budgetary constraints, how could they recruit desperately needed additional personnel without aggravating the "advancement crisis"? A greater reliance on women, already tested in urban telegraph and telephone bureaus, seemed to provide an answer. Despite the low wages and lack of real promotional prospects, the position offered women most of the relative advantages already experienced by *receveuses*. There was, therefore, no shortage of candidates: in an 1889 examination held in Paris for telegraph employment, 614 women had competed for 82

openings and in a national *concours* in 1893, 5,600 women would
vie for 400 positions.[51] In view of the "advancement crisis" of men
clerks, the advantages women employees offered for filling dead-
end jobs were clear. As André Froüin, assistant to the personnel
director, told future postal administrators at the *Ecole professionnelle supérieure des postes* a few years later: "Today there exists a
category of employees who resemble in some ways the auxiliary
clerks of old. These are the *dames employées.* They have the same
duties as clerks but they cannot aspire to chief clerk positions."
"The feminization," he explained, "is a convenient means of giv-
ing men clerks greater chances of advancement. The number of men
employees are less numerous and the number of supervisory positions tend to increase; it is clear, therefore, that men clerks can
more easily attain the position of chief clerk."[52] Regardless of the
exact job they held—post office clerk, telegraph or telephone
operator—all women were to be hired in the separate female grade
of *dame employée.* All *dames employées* would have the same wage
scale and compete for promotion only with women on a separate
female career ladder.

A turn to employing more women seemed even more imperative
in view of what was happening in the countryside. Owing to the
tightened budget, few new local post offices were being established.[53] While the opportunities for *aides* were diminishing on this
front, the passage of a new military law in 1889 threatened to take
existing appointments away from *aides* in favor of the appointment
of former non-commissioned officers.[54] Generally, the large
number of women competing for appointments reflected the fact
that women's schooling had progressed at a much faster pace than
new employment opportunities for the educated women. In this
climate, the Postal Administration was being "overwhelmed by
demands, supported energetically by numerous senators, deputies"
to open more jobs to women.[55] Jules Roche, Minister of Commerce
and Posts, stated publicly on the floor of the Chamber of Deputies in
1891 that he had "applied [himself] to the task of increasing opportunities for women" because he believed "it a question of utmost
social importance to procure situations for women permitting them
to live honorably."[56] Roche's successor, Jules Siegfried, had to
have agreed with these sentiments if he paid any attention to the activities of his wife, a prominent figure in Parisian feminist circles.

Once having decided to place women clerks in urban post offices,
administrators drew up a plan of bureaus where women would

work. The choice reflected several criteria. First, there were considerations involving the physical layout of the bureau. Since the personnel in any post office would be, to a limited extent at least, mixed by sex, administrators sought to place women in bureaus where there would be a "real separation between men and women employees, notably with regard to the cloakroom and accessory premises." In some instances this meant modifying existing post offices: the 1892 report of the Director General of Postal Services included mention of funds expended to modify the premises of eight post offices in Paris "to allow ladies to take over the services."[57] Second, care was taken in the selection of the neighborhoods where women were to work. Administrators avoided introducing women into post offices neighboring railroad stations, since they considered the busyness of such locales unsuited to women's "natural nervousness."[58]

The first two "test" post offices where women began to work in May 1892 were located in quiet residential neighborhoods, removed from the busy commercial center, one in Passy in the 16th Arrondissement and the other on the rue de la Glacière, on the edge of the 14th.[59] Presumably it was by design that these post offices were located in "better," generally bourgeois, neighborhoods. The Passy post office was the local post office for Director General of Postal Services, Justin de Selves.[60] Between the end of 1892 and late 1893, administrators placed women in sixteen additional bureaus dispersed over twelve different Arrondissements. Only one of the post offices was newly established. Women's employment remained foreign to certain parts of Paris, notably such working-class neighborhoods as Belleville (19th) and La Villette (20th). All but one of the first twenty bureaus in which women were placed belonged to the smallest, fourth class of urban post offices.

Since administrators sought to minimize the moral dangers associated with women's employment, the first women actually introduced into post offices in Paris were far from impressionable young women. They were not, as one writer falsely claimed, between the ages of eighteen and twenty-five, the legal age for first appointment as a *dame employée*. Employee records show that though most women (86 percent) in the first group were single, their average age was twenty-eight. Only one in five was under twenty-five years old and no woman was under twenty-one. Nor were these women novices to postal work. Most had generally worked five to ten years as urban telegraph employees or *aides* in provincial post offices. *Aides* born in the provinces predominated, representing about three of four of the new urban employees; they were drawn from thirty-eight different departments and had probably been the *aides* ranked highest on departmental lists for *receveuse* appointments. The minority of Parisians had worked in the telegraph central and usually ran the telegraph in the neighborhood bureau. The first contingent of women to work in post office no. 62 on the avenue de la Grande Armée in the summer of 1892 included: the Parisian, Mlle Madeleine Samouel (twenty-seven years old), and provincial *aides,* Mlles Louise Léger (twenty-six), Marie Perrin (twenty-seven), Suzanne Rappe (twenty-six), Amélie Azéma (twenty-nine), Marie Juste (twenty-seven), and Anne Borreau (twenty-eight) born respectively in the departments of the Ariège, Manche, Somme, Tarn, Yonne, and Côte d'Or.

From 1892 through early 1894, women were also placed in provincial post offices, and the employment of women in telegraph centrals stepped up. About forty provincial post offices were affected. The first targeted cities were less important administrative or commercial centers on the order of Ambérieu (Ain) and Ambert (Puy-de-Dôme). Subsequently, however, women were also placed in the capitals of some departments, including Clermont-Ferrand, Bourges, Versailles, Angoulême, Moulins, Poitiers, and neighborhood post offices in Bordeaux. Women's employment in telegraph centrals was extended to cities such as Caen, Rouen, Montpellier, Le Mans, Dijon, and Limoges. At the same time, the proportion of women employed in the Paris telegraph central was increasing. What is more, for the first time a small number of women climbed the stairs to the men's work room to learn how to operate the Baudot telegraph, a machine formerly operated only by men.

In this way, the experiment using women in urban post offices, introduced with "a timid hand in the discreet shadow of a post office where the *receveur* had been won over to the idea" took on, in a very short period of time, much wider dimensions.[61] The magnitude of the change and increasing public visibility of the women employees in the cities provoked wide comment in the Paris and provincial press as well as mounting alarm in the postal employee journals. As the recruitment of men clerks was all but halted, writers began to use the term *"feminisation,"* placed in italics to indicate the novelty of the expression, to describe the substitution of women for men. For critics of the policy, the term had pejorative connotations synomous with *"emasculation."*

FIGURE 3. Feminized Post Office in the Paris Suburb of Le Perreux (c. 1900). *Receveur* is at far left, and the chief mail carrier next to him. The *dames employées* stand in a group slightly apart. (Courtesy of Musée de la Poste)

45

Chapter Four:
Reactions to the Feminization Policy:
Image and Reality

The premiere appearance of women in post offices in Paris and other cities received mixed reviews. In the pages of *L'Illustration* and the stage of a Montmartre cabaret, jokes and satire abounded on the possibilities for romantic and sexual encounters between *dames employées* and the men who frequented their bureaus.[1] A writer for the journal *L'Eclair* voiced another common reaction when he applauded the public's opportunity "to contemplate, through the light grille of the counter windows, the pleasant faces of young *postières.*"[2] Attempting to capitalize on the prurient interest in the personal lives of the women, the central administration clerk Albert Cim put the woman employee at the center of his popular novel, *Marriageable Young Ladies (Demoiselles à Marier),* published in 1894, which feminists were quick to denounce for its negative stereotypical portrait.[3]

A surprising number of more serious commentators in the Paris press hailed the innovation. "The business of this great administration (the Postal Services) with the public calls for qualities native to women," was the comment proffered in the popular daily *Le Petit Journal:* "Sweetness, patience, resignation; you will never find all three in a man." In the same writer's opinion, the measure opened an opportunity for girls who "aspire only to gain their independence." He concluded that it was "the duty of the state" to continue the feminization "to its limits."[4] A writer for *La Paix* concurred: "The innovation which has been adopted offers steady and suitable employment for a large number of girls and young women who have difficulty finding . . . remunerative work." "Besides," the writer added, "for a long time women have proven generally capable of this kind of occupation, and many of them may be found in the provinces under the title *[receveuse] des postes.*"[5]

Parisian feminists were most pleased by the change. Particularly delighted was the group *La Solidarité des Femmes,* which had been

LES DEMOISELLES DANS LES BUREAUX DE POSTE
— Où demeurez-vous, monsieur?
— Rue Greneta, 247, sur le devant, à l'entresol à droite... J'y suis toujours dans l'après-midi., Et vous?...

FIGURE 4. Cartoon from *L'Illustration*. When the lady asks the gentleman his address, he provides it, including the floor, and adds that he is home every afternoon. "And you?" he then asks. (Courtesy of Musée de la Poste)

founded just one year earlier by Eugénie Potonié-Pierre with the aid of Maria Martin, editor of *Le Journal des Femmes*. In contrast to the timid and legalistic feminism which was typical around 1890, *La Solidarité* represented an original attempt to "create a feminism distinct from socialism but responsive to the social question, particularly in regard to working women."[6] Among the group's first

concrete actions was their effort to lobby the Postal Administration
in 1891 for the employment of women as *receveuses* in urban post
offices. Considering that such management positions consituted a
promotional opportunity for clerks, and in view of the "advancement crisis," *La Solidarité's* desire to see women manage urban
post offices was singularly inopportune (and has not been fulfilled to
the present day). Still, in seeing women employed as clerks in urban
bureaus, the group was at least partly satisfied, indeed rewarded, in
their opinion, for their efforts. "We consider," it was announced at
a group meeting, "that we have played some part in this forward
movement." *La Solidarité* sent several letters to Director General
Selves thanking him "for the widening scope every day to the
feminization of post offices in Paris." "In this way," the group
noted, "you come to aid . . . in the most practical fashion our work
of emancipation."[7]

But the major postal employee journals, normally sectarian
rivals, united in vigorous, enduring opposition to the feminization
policy. The pro-administration *La Revue des Postes* announced the
news of personnel changes for every affected bureau frequently adding editorial comment indicating, albeit in a respectful tone, its
disapproval of the policy.[8] Pierre Farjanel, the editor of *Le Journal
des Postes,* tried to whip up sentiment against the measure in exaggerated bombastic fashion. One of the early leaders in efforts to
organize postal employees in the 1880s and a former *receveur des
postes* at the post office in the Chamber of Deputies, Farjanel called
women's employment as post office clerks "most immoral and anti-
social": "I have the greatest confidence in the courtesy of the male
[chief] clerks who will supervise the work, but nonetheless avow
that this promiscuity is a challenge to human weakness, an encouragement to free love, to the bestial instinct."[9] The new socialist
journal, *L'Union des Postes,* also objected strongly to the measure:
"For the sake of the sound execution of services and of humanity
and morality, we protest with all our energy against the intrusion of
women into post offices in Paris and the large cities; [this measure]
reflects the reign of imbecillity, the absolute triumph of administrative cretinism."[10] During 1893 and 1894, at the height of the feminization policy, scarcely an issue of these three journals appeared
without some discussion of the question. Frequently a single issue
contained several news stories, commentaries, as well as letters
from readers on the subject. The reaction, which would continue up
to the end of the century, was overwhelmingly hostile, as writers
used a range of tactics and arguments to discredit the measure.

The tone and content of the discussion resembled in some respects the treatment women had received in the 1840s from *La France Administrative.* A common ploy exaggerated isolated cases of "scandalous" behavior by women employees. For example, the story of a "coquette" *dame employée* whose chief clerk was brought to court by her husband for "an attempt of assault on his property," was told and retold in various forms.[11] While the women's intelligence was not doubted as much as it had been fifty years earlier, writers at the end of the century still questioned women's abilities to perform the work as well as men. Women were either too "shy," too "slow," too "nervous," or too "weak":

> At certain moments of the day, notably before the evening mail collection, the counter windows are crowded, assaulted by an impatient, hurried public . . . At these times, a male employee, no matter how agile, cannot always succeed in satisfying these hurried and surging customers . . . But you want to impose on women, on girls, this nervous irritation so trying that a strong person cannot escape it? What illogicalness, what an aberration![12]

Another frequent assertion claimed that any savings won from the employment of women at lower salaries than men was illusory, since the amount of work done by one woman was less than that done by one man. In recounting the replacement of male clerks by higher numbers of *dames employées* in certain bureaus these writers chose to ignore that administrators had conceived of the feminization of jobs in part as a means of increasing the personnel and thereby alleviating the problem of long waits in post offices.[13] That the pride of men employees was partly at stake in the 1890s just as it had been in the 1840s seems even more evident in less subtle declarations, such as one that expressed outrage that "the sale of stamps in Paris" ever be equated to "the peddling of the Salvation Army journal."[14]

In the 1890s, however, employment as *receveuse,* work for which women had once also been deemed unsuited, became the ideal against which women's work in urban post offices was set. "We understand very well that a woman makes an excellent *receveuse* in a small locality," one writer remarked. "She can work with composure; but in an office in Paris, a veritable furnace!"[15] In small post offices when the *receveuse* is confused [about rates or procedures], she has time to leaf through the [instructions] manual,'' another commentator observed. "But in Paris when a *dame* has fifteen impatient and irritable persons in front of her, she will well have the time to search for answers to diverse questions!"[16] "In the rural post offices . . . a woman is fit for the work while in the urban bureaus, in a milieu of male personnel and contacts with a noisy, strange, and large public, a woman is displaced to say the least," yet another writer claimed.[17]

Critics of the feminization policy, like the opponents of women's introduction into industrial and artisanal trades, evoked a domestic ideology restricting woman's place to the home. The feminization policy, they claimed, betrayed the traditional role of woman as wife and mother and contributed to the further decline of France's low birthrate.[18] Writers placed the blame alternately on the administration for "uprooting woman from the home," on the misguided development of girls' education, and on the woman herself whose education "had awakened in her a certain ambition and then, little by little, a disturbing distaste for the work of her sex."[19] Some writers even referred disdainfully to the women as "egoistic boys" or "bluestockings."[20]

PROFILE OF THE DAME EMPLOYÉE

The typical writer's view had little basis in reality and polemicists cared minimally about truth. Although some more subtle writers conceded that women were forced to work for economic reasons, they did not find this sufficient to support the feminization policy. In fact, all the evidence supports the view, admitted by one critic, who explained that girls whose "most ardent desire" was to marry but who had no dowries were compelled, in order to live, to make a situation for themselves."[21]

Aides whose modest social orgins have been described (and as shown in Table 1)[22] would continue throughout the 1890s and early 1900s to fill most positions as *dames employées,* whether in postal, telegraph, or telephone work. Many having spent their late teen years and early twenties working as auxiliaries in small provincial bureaus, more than two of three (69 percent) of the group of provincial birth were twenty-three years old or more on becoming urban *dames employées.* Women recruited locally in Paris and other cities of employment were as a group younger—only one-third of those born in Paris over twenty-three—and they also tended to be better educated. But these women of urban origins who had never been

Table 1.   Fathers' Occupations of *Dames Employées* Born in
             Selected Departments before 1876 (percentages)*

	Department of Birth		
	Nord	Gironde	Hérault
Father's Occupation	(n = 186)	(n = 71)	(n = 82)
Lawyer, other "professional"	-	1.4	3.6
Large businessman, manager	3.2	9.9	7.1
Small shopkeeper	17.7	12.7	14.3
White-collar postal employee	3.2	2.8	3.6
Mail carrier	2.2	1.4	10.7
Captain, other military officer	3.8	1.4	3.6
Police, non-commissioned military	9.1	-	10.7
Schoolteacher, other educator	1.1	4.2	3.6
Other civil servant	4.3	9.8	-
Accountant, other office employee	3.7	1.4	7.2
Transportation employee	2.7	4.2	7.1
Commerce employee	7.6	2.8	-
Artisan	26.9	32.4	7.1
Unskilled worker	3.2	1.4	-
Domestic servant, other service	2.2	2.8	-
Cultivator	7.6	7.0	17.9
Property-owner, rentier	1.6	4.2	3.6
	100%	100%	100%

*When available, mother's occupation was used if father's occupation was unknown.

aides also came from modest petit-bourgeois or working-class
backgrounds, and with the expansion of jobs, proportionately higher
numbers of Parisians of humbler social origin entered employment
(see Table 2). There were no formal diploma requirements, and the
entrance examination tested only matters of a solid primary school
education. Women with teaching diplomas continued to be favored
in the selection process, however: an estimated one-fourth to one-
half of all applicants had diplomas in the early 1890s.[23]

Clearly, whatever their specific backgrounds, few women chose
postal employment out of a yearning for independence. This was
true even for *employees* of more bourgeois origins, who, like the
receveuses of old, were *déclassées* whose families would have
preferred to keep them in their homes. Marie Ancelin, for example,
was a graduate of the prestigious Sacré Coeur and the daughter of a
commercial broker. Upon her application for postal work, her

Table 2.　　Fathers' Occupations of *Dames Employées*
Born in Paris before 1876 (percentages)

Father's Occupation	Women Born Before 1865 (n = 283)	Women Born 1865-1875 (n = 671)	All (n = 954)
Lawyer, other "professional"	1.8	0.6	0.9
Writer, artist	1.8	1.2	1.4
Large businessman, manager	3.5	1.9	2.4
Small shopkeeper	13.8	16.8	15.9
White-collar postal employee	5.7	5.7	5.7
Mail carrier	1.4	3.7	3.0
Captain, other military officer	3.2	0.7	1.5
Police, non-commissioned military	6.0	3.1	4.0
Schoolteacher, other educator	3.2	0.7	1.5
Other civil servant	4.6	3.4	3.8
Accountant, other office employee	3.2	4.6	4.2
Commerce or unspecified employee	17.0	17.3	17.2
Artisan	23.3	31.4	29.0
Unskilled worker	2.5	2.2	2.3
Domestic servant, other service	7.4	5.8	6.3
Property-owner, rentier	1.8	0.6	0.9
	100%	100%	100%

parents felt compelled to state that "necessities and disappointments of life had forced them to place her in employment" and that the measure was hopefully only "provisory."[24] Some of Mlle Ancelin's cohorts, generally of less privileged upbringings, saw postal employment as a less desirable alternative to schoolteaching, a profession which began in the 1880s to enjoy higher esteem and better remuneration. But the formidable competition in the field and the longer requisite schooling stood in the way of some women who eventually became *dames employées*. Marie Louise Baudré, for example, had been forced to leave her teacher-training school for postal employment after the death of her father, a mail carrier, had left her family in financial straits.[25] Even greater numbers of women saw postal work as a decidedly more desirable alternative to employment in the garment trades. They included women like Mathilde De Than, the daughter of modest landowners, who, having worked in her home town for seven years as an *aide* after receiving her primary school certificate, entered telegraph work in the city of Caen in 1892, married in 1893, and remained employed until her retirement in 1930; and Mlle Bernard, the daughter of a ship carpenter and café keeper, who, while she worked as an *aide,* had prepared for the examination for *dames employées* through correspondence courses.[26]

The relative attraction of postal employment can be seen in the occupations of applicants for the very first positions ever to open in the departments of Calvados and Hérault in the early 1890s. At the time of the examination, 26 percent of the women were *aides,* 12 percent were employed in the sewing trades, 12 percent were private teachers or tutors, 9 percent were shop employees, and 37 percent were listed as "students" or "unemployed, at home."[27] Reflecting both their modest backgrounds and the narrow range of employment options open to women in the capital, almost 26 percent of *dames employées* born in Paris had mothers listed on their birth records as "seamstress" or other garment worker. Another 10 percent had mothers who were domestic servants and concierges, 9 percent shopkeepers, and 8 percent other manual workers. Only 3 percent of the Parisians had mothers listed as schoolteacher or other white-collar employee.

Moreover, though nine of ten *dames employées* were single upon appointment and many never married, this scarcely implied, as some writers suggested, that these women, any more than earlier generations of *receveuses,* had rejected the ideal of marriage and family. Of every three *dames employées* who were single upon entering the work force, one left for marriage or other reasons, one married and remained in the work force, and one did not marry at all and remained working. Of the significant minority of women who remained single, some women, like the modern heroine of Alfred Capus's play *La Petite Fonctionnaire* (1904), refused to pity themselves because they had no dowry for marriage and rejected the pity of others. Real life examples were some of the militantly feminist editors of the journal *L'Union des Dames de la Poste* (1900-1908), whose opinions we will encounter in a later chapter. But unmarried women in at least equal numbers must have suffered from the social stigma of being old maids. Apparently, like the *receveuses* before them, most *dames employées* who remained single did so because of the constraints imposed by social convention rather than any philosophical rejection of marriage.

Dames employées who did marry almost universally married men in white-collar jobs. Thus, about one of three *dames employées* in Paris who married at the end of the century married men employed in the postal services administration, and 83 percent of all those who married in Paris during this period married white-collar employees in either the public or private sector. The pattern was similar in a city like Bordeaux.[28] The pool of suitable marriage partners was limited by the unwillingness of middle-class men to marry working women and women without dowries, and by the aspirations of women themselves, whose education and upbringing made them aim higher than their financial resources allowed. Women from Paris married, as a group, at a younger age than women from the provinces—over half by age twenty-seven, compared to twenty-eight-and-a-half for provincials. But though many Parisians lived with their families and theoretically had greater opportunities for saving for a dowry, their marriage rate was not higher than those in other areas. Finally, despite the employees' high rate of celibacy, the women who began their employment as *dames employées* still married more easily than those who had started as *receveuses* employed in a domestic setting.[29]

It is true that despite their modest backgrounds compared to previous generations of *receveuses,* the women who became civil servants in the Postal Administration still represented a rather privileged group among female wage earners in the late nineteenth century. Many poorer families could not afford to have their daughters continue schooling after the age of thirteen. Others could not obey the law for obligatory attendance because their daughter's wages, however slim, were essential. As short as the two month or so apprenticeship period for *dame employée* was, it was sufficiently burdensome, particularly if done away from home to prevent many women's applications.[30] Since the entrance examination was given only in the departmental capitals, application there involved the costs of transportation and usually an overnight stay, which were prohibitive for some women. Yet, the need to work for a living was no less imperative for the women who did become *dames employées.* They simply had greater means of escaping the usual female fields of employment.

THE PROBLEM OF COMPETITION

Even when the fact of women's economic need was admitted, few critics were willing to allow women to compete freely with men for work, particularly in jobs long considered and reaffirmed as ''men's work." Just as Frenchmen in the metallurgical trades, to cite one example, had responded to women's competition by relegating them "to the family and needle trades" or "to the family and textile work," men postal employees and their spokesmen were adept at finding more "suitable" alternatives to urban postal employment for the better-educated woman.

There was saleswork, for example: "A woman is an excellent saleswoman; she has one hundred charming turns of phrase to entice the buyer, but when it is a question of a public service, we have no time to care about her smiles."[31] There was schoolteaching: "The schoolteacher fulfills a role very compatible with the faculties of a woman; the upbringing and education of children may be confided to her with advantage . . . , but to open wide to her the doors of our administrations means ruining her physically and morally, compromising the execution of services, and obstructing the already difficult access to the careers for today's male youth."[32] And, of course, there was the position of *receveuse* within the Postal Administration. A movement began to abrogate the law designating an important proportion of these positions for non-commissioned officers: "Until the present . . . it had been justly thought that the simplicity of the work . . . suited [women's] aptitudes and that through this work they would be assured a peaceful and moral means of support in small centers where they could at once uphold their administrative duties, the management of the household and care of the family."[33] Even if one discounts the obviously idealized images of the work of saleswoman, schoolteacher, or *receveuse des postes,* it is evident that such suggestions, aimed at maintaining occupational segregation by sex, failed dismally to provide a solution to the problem of competition between men and women for work. Women were already over-crowded in the hypothetical alternative fields.

The extent to which opposition to the feminization policy reflected a real concern for the material interests of men already employed as clerks is more difficult to ascertain. In industrial trades the employment of women at lower salaries raised legitimate fears that men's salaries would be undercut, their jobs threatened, and efforts at unionization undermined.[34] These concerns were echoed only faintly in the postal employee journals. Objections over salary undercutting could scarcely have been expected from the ranks of the "auxiliary clerks" who had just seen their situations upgraded. Indeed, the savings won from employing women, legislators stated publicly more than once, had been used to finance this very amelioration.[35] Moreover, the job security of all clerks, as civil servants, was assured. A second, more convincing objection involved the displacement of clerks, particularly in lesser provincial centers, to other cities because of the feminization of their post offices. The fear of displacement, even if unfounded, had a psychological effect.[36] A related fear was that male clerks, in face of a continuing feminization of post offices, would be left only with the least desirable jobs, such as sorting mail.[37]

But a minority of writers made equally convincing arguments that the feminization policy facilitated the promotions of clerks. One clerk who signed his letter "a former blocked clerk promoted to chief clerk thanks to the feminization" asserted his support for the change on this very ground.[38] The "advancement crisis" affecting men clerks had in fact eased by 1896. Between 1890 and 1898, the proportion of clerks to chief clerks had fallen. Through the combined reliance on *dames employées* and a raise in the maximum salary for clerks, the average interval between raises had dropped for clerks from a high of four years, eleven months in 1890 to three years, three months during the period from 1892 to 1898.[39] In 1892 the demand for regular advancement was at the top of the list of reforms proposed by the editor of *L'Union des Postes,* but that demand was not even on the list of reforms proposed in 1898.[40] Thus, if the feminization of urban services had the effect of limiting men's demands it was not because it threatened men's jobs but because it brought about a relative improvement in clerks' situation. That postal clerks never struck to protest the introduction of women, as did a fair number of industrial workers, does not so much reflect an absence of militancy as an absence of desperation.

Still, whether or not clerks perceived the feminization policy as a way to improve their material situation, the psychological effect of seeing a sudden, sizeable influx of women into the postal services must have been considerable. The "out and out feminization" *(feminisation à outrance),* as the policy came to be called, was an accurate expression for a measure which saw the number of female employees in urban postal and telegraph services combined more than triple between 1890 and 1898 and over the same period the absolute number of clerks fall.[41] After the protests over blocked advancement in the late 1880s and early 1890s, the feminization policy may have been felt as insult heaped on injury. And after the first hard confrontation with administrators, the balance of power had been modified to the extent that the clerks and the employee journals were well prepared to be outspoken in their criticism of administration policies. These factors, in addition to the historical identification of post office clerking positions with men, and the sometimes frightening, wider social and cultural implications of the change, help explain why opposition to women's introduction into urban post offices was more intense in the 1890s than in the previous decade, when women entered telegraph and telephone employment. The question remained, though: What impact would critics have on the administrators who set recruitment policies and on legislators who surveyed the administration's budget?

Chapter Five:
Politics and the Feminization Policy

In their public statements postal administrators appeared un-moved by protests over the feminization policy. In November 1893, for example, a spokesman declared to the press that "behind our postal counter windows, our women employees are able to satisfy the public just as well as men employees." He warned the public against prejudging the women.[1] Some *receveurs,* managers of feminized bureaus, publicly concurred. Said one: "Far from having to complain about these *demoiselles,* I can only praise them." He reported that the women employees' "indispositions" were less fre-quent than sometimes charged by critics and their morality "above all reproach."[2] Another *receveur* wrote that he found in his women employees "a submissiveness, much goodwill, and in some . . . a training not possessed by the auxiliaries and apprentice clerks who had usually comprised the personnel of our bureaus."[3]

Lacking autonomy in budgetary decisions, the administration's hardest task was to convince the politically sensitive Chamber of Deputies of the policy's wisdom in the face of mounting opposition. To this end, it produced justifications that related only obliquely to the initial reasons for the feminization of urban services. In the 1894 budget, for example, the administration was obliged to explain its motives for requesting credits to transform "a combined 768 or-dinary and auxiliary clerks into 1,057 *dames employées.*" To rally support, spokesmen cited the fifteen years of experience with women in urban telegraph, telephone, and administrative services and described the results of this employment as "conclusive," "very satisfactory." The administration evoked, secondarily, "the problem of the *aides.*" For reasons of "humanity," the postal employer had sought to create new positions for these young women. Finally, the administration argued that owing to "a preoc-cupation to assure normal services in case of mobilization . . . the assistance of ladies became imperative in order that the service not be jeopardized."[4]

A few undiscerning and uninformed listeners accepted these

statements at face value. For example, the pro-government *La Paix* urged the public to be patient with the innovation and appealed to their patriotic sentiments by repeating the administration's apparent concern for military preparedness.[5] It is possible that preparation for mobilization was a minor contributing cause of the feminization: *conseil d'administration* minutes for the postal administraion in the late 1880s reveal a general awareness of the eventuality of war, and Justin de Selves, Director General of Postal Services (1890-1896) was the cousin of Freycinet, the Minister of War from 1892 to 1893.[6] Some writers argued, however, that the feminization policy was actually a threat to military preparedness because of the need to have ready sufficient male employees for military telegraph services, the Treasury office, and army postal services.[7] In any case, the administration's evasiveness in hiding the material advantages of using women in urban bureaus and *aides* in rural offices was evident, and writers justifiably denounced such public statement as post-facto rationalizations.[8]

The administration also failed to win the unqualified support of the Chamber of Deputies. Representing a range of political affiliations, legislators who scrutinized the postal budget gave the policy only carefully circumscribed approval at best. In its report for 1894, the budgetary committee could find no reason to oppose the policy. But the authors of the report admitted in the two pages devoted to the measure that "the experience with regard to services where there was public contact [that is, post offices] was still incomplete" and urged the administration "not to proceed hastily in the transformation":

> While recognizing that it is legitimate to open administrative careers to women, the committee would point out that certain positions are more suited to them than others. Thus positions as *receveuses* which permit them to maintain their family life, to take care of their household, are more preferable than administrative functions in bureaus of large cities.[9]

But the feminization policy was extended, so the following year the budgetary committee looked more closely at the measure. Five pages including statistics were devoted to the subject. Here the legislators recognized that "many women had shown qualities of intelligence, zeal, and energy in assuring postal services, even in some of the busiest bureaus," while "others, less able, ought to be kept in secondary locales.'' On the question of women's contact with the public, the committee members were surprisingly positive, declaring that ''the transformation had not given rise to any serious complaints.'' But this generally positive assessment was undercut in the final conclusion: while applauding the savings realized by the employment of women, the committee feared that the economic advantage might be nullified if female employees continued, as critics observed, to take more sickdays than men.[10]

The budgetary report for 1895, which devoted eight pages to the feminization policy, sought to confirm that women took a disproportionate number of sickdays: its statistics showed that nationally, for all services, women took an average of 33.5 days annually compared to 19.2 days for men.[11] While the report offered no analysis of the possible reasons for the difference, other evidence suggested that it was the most physically demanding work in cramped telephone bureaus which produced an inordinate number of illnesses among women employees as a group in Paris.[12] In the meantime, the administration admitted that absences due to ''indispositions'' were a ''little more numerous'' for women than for men but asserted that they had anticipated this situation.[13] The truthfulness of the statement in this instance seems borne out by evidence which shows that an awareness of women's tendency to take a higher number of sickdays existed in administrative circles even before the feminization policy, in the 1880s.

In parliamentary discussions socialist deputies, members of the opposition, stood out in their criticism of the measure. While they shared prevalent attitudes and prejudices regarding ''woman's place,'' their expression of these views in a public forum was expedient, given their constituency of working-class men fearful of competition from women. In a meeting of the Chamber of Deputies in February 1895, deputies Arthur Groussier *(Allemaniste)* and Rene Chauvin *(Parti ouvrier français)* invoked the social and moral consequences of women's work outside the home. ''Is it under the pretext that women are cheaper than men thatone ought . . . to replace men by women in our administrations?'' deputy Groussier demanded. ''This trend, which also exists in industry, even in the metal trades, is absolutely baneful,'' he continued, ''especially considering that unemployment becomes more and more considerable.'' He was willing, when pressed, to consider the traditionally acceptable employment of women without support, that is, widows or unmarried women, but he held it unacceptable that ''one attempt to uproot the wife from the *foyer* to replace man in his work.''[15] That most female employees were single upon entrance into postal employment escaped him. Groussier reiterated his remarks to applause on the floor in late 1896.[16] No one defended the feminization policy in the Chamber.

The only individuals and organizations supporting the feminization policy with a fervor equal to that of its opponents were Parisian feminists. The outstanding example was Hubertine Auclert (1848-1914), the leading advocate of women's suffrage in France and one of the most brilliant orators ever enlisted in the cause.[17] Just as she had defended women's introduction into the printing trades in 1883, Auclert came, in 1894, to the defense of the *postières*. While recognizing the exploitation of women in the administraton, she refused to let this serve, in the way it did for critics, as a pretext for the elimination of women from employment. ''From the unimportant to the important, all postal employees are closing ranks at the arrival of women,'' she wrote. ''Does not the public complain continually and with reason, about the male personnel? But in this instance, discontent goes unnoticed, the manager of the bureau covers for his sex.'' Auclert went on to argue that the stories in the press of women falling ill in post offices reminded her of ''omnibus horses, much stronger than women, which nevertheless fall into the stretcher when their ration of oats is cut short.'' Finally, the suffragist Auclert suggested that less unfairness would be shown women if they had representatives in the legislature who defended their interests and demanded the same salary for them as men for the same work: ''Women are not electors, so naturally no deputy can take the side against the clerks who vote, of the female clerks who do not.''[18]

Joining the voice of Auclert were those of members of the continually loyal *La Solidarité des Femmes,* joined by the *Ligue Française pour le droit des Femmes.* On the pages of *Le Journal des Femmes,* these feminists refuted notions, such as those advanced by the eminent economist Paul Leroy-Beaulieu, that ''the intellectualization of women,'' manifested by women's employment in schoolteaching, the postal service, and other state administrations contributed to depopulation.[19]

Neither the worst fears of feminists nor the highest hopes of their opponents were realized. Women were not to be chased from the post offices into the streets, and all post offices were not to be ''defeminized.'' But neither did the feminization of jobs progress in linear fashion as later writers maintained.[20] Instead, 'in the late

1890s, the feminization of post offices came to a slow halt. Yet, as late as 1896, the administration was still stating publicly that "the experiment had succeeded perfectly . . . the women placed in bureaus of lesser importance . . . as well as those introduced into offices of greater importance . . . had performed admirably the task confided them."[21] Was the administration simply trying to save face by refusing to admit the drawbacks of the feminization policy, as some critics suggested? Or was the shift in policy a reflection of new leadership in the administration? The continuity of leadership provided by Director General Selves ended in 1896 when he left the position to become prefect of the department of the Seine. There were doubtlessly disagreements over feminization in central administration offices, just as some *receveurs* opposed the feminization policy while others approved of it, and just as departmental directors divided over the issue.[22] In Selves' absence, opponents may have become more outspoken.

Administrators' sensitivity to criticism even during the Selves' administration becomes apparent after a close examination of the post offices in Paris where women worked by 1900. By then, only thirty-six of the 100 post offices in Paris had women employees. Five bureaus originally feminized no longer employed women (the result of objections?) which meant that altogether only twenty-one bureaus had been feminized over the period from 1894 to 1900, that is, after the original wave of feminizations. Thirty-two of the thirty-six bureaus where women worked in 1900 were in the smallest, fourth-class category (which totalled sixty-six). Almost no women worked in post offices which had late evening hours or were located in central commercial Arrondissements (1-6).[23] This suggests that by 1900, fully eight years after the initial execution of the feminization policy, the administration still considered the matter a sufficiently "delicate" problem that it had ventured little beyond the scope of the original plan.

The appointment of Alexandre Millerand as Minister of Commerce, Industry and Postal Services in 1899 boded poorly for the future of the measure. In the early 1890s Millerand had edited *La petite République,* a socialist journal outspoken in the defense of male postal employees' interests and an opponent, from the beginning, of the feminization policy.[24] In a long report on postal services published in May 1900, Millerand renounced future feminizations of bureaus. Describing "the infatuation born in 1893 for the so-called feminization," Millerand summarized all the arguments previously used against women's employment in urban bureaus. He concluded that women were "not cut out for the service to which they had been admitted," a service that required "a *sang-froid* not always found to a sufficient degree in the female personnel." In his view, women were more naturally suited for work as *receveuse,* a position permitting them to have an "honorable career without separating them from the *foyer.* "[25] His pronouncement carried such weight that his words were echoed in reports, articles and books published from 1900 to 1914.[26]

A decade after Millerand's speech women were still working in the same bureaus as in 1900, but few new post offices had been feminized.[27] Before the war women never worked in neighborhood post offices with the heaviest mail volume and largest concentration of clerks nor in the main post offices of Paris and the major provincial cities.

When one weighs the advantages of female labor against the disadvantages, it is hard to believe that Millerand's decision was based on a careful calculation of these factors. Even though women took more sickdays, this drawback was offset by women's greater experience and maturity, compared to the younger, inexperienced male clerks usually placed in urban post offices, by the larger pool of better-educated, cheaper female labor, and by the unique role women played in filling low-level jobs without clamoring for promotion to the chief clerk rank and higher. That Millerand had taken a stand against the feminization of post offices from the moment of the policy's introduction further suggests the importance political considerations played in his decision: whether or not he believed what he said, his position was politically opportune given his particular Parisian constituency, which included Parisian postal clerks, and his wider support in labor ranks. Millerand had not waited to evaluate women's performance and, had he done so, it hardly would have been with an open mind. The same may be said of many other critics of the policy.

To be fair, one would have to point out that the arguments of feminist proponents also revealed a certain distance from the actual events and the men and women employees involved. Each side's goal, above all, was to score polemical points in the name of the sex whose interests they tried either to safeguard or promote.

That Millerand's view held sway reflected in part the even greater organized power of postal clerks after 1900. In that year the first association for white-collar employees, *L'Association générale des Agents,* was established. The extreme sensitivity with which the Parisian deputy Marcel Sembat, an ally of the association and

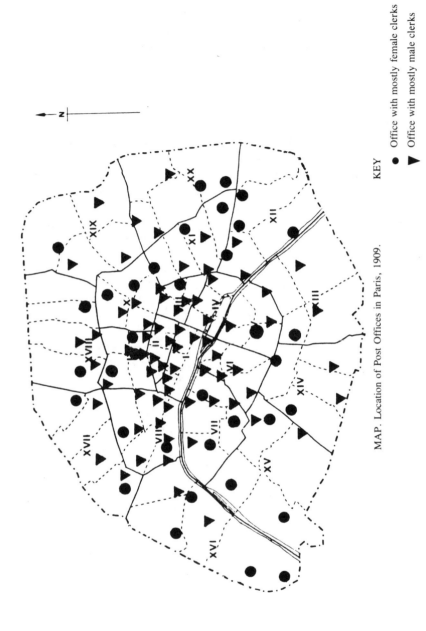

MAP. Location of Post Offices in Paris, 1909.

KEY

● Office with mostly female clerks

▶ Office with mostly male clerks

Susan Bachrach 65

himself a *postier's* son, broached the subject of *dames employées* and new openings in his budgetary reports (1901-1906) suggests that the administration might have encountered even greater opposition if it had tried furthering the feminization policy.[28] On the other side, no concerted effort was mounted by feminists to broaden the opportunities for women in the administration after 1900. Women were more concerned with winning a coveted appointment. Or, once in the administration, they sought to improve their immediate material situation. Considering their weak position in the economy and the body politic, women were no match for their opponents. After 1900, postal administrators continued to face the same problems that had plagued them during the 1880s and 1890s: personnel shortages, career blockages of clerks, the problem of the *aides*. But a greater reliance on women in urban services was no longer viewed, before the war, as a viable solution to these labor problems.

The end to an explicit feminization policy meant that in the decade before the war there was little further integration by sex of the work force. It is true that the proportion of *dames employées* in all postal, telegraph, and telephone services combined increased slightly over-all, relative to clerks (Table 3). But this change reflected the fact that telephone services, in both Paris and the pro-

Table 3. Clerks and *Dames Employées* by Service, 1902, 1911

| | 1902 | | | 1911 | | |
Service	Clerks	Dames	Dames-% of Total	Clerks	Dames	Dames-% of Total
Paris-Telegraph	782	725	48.1%	975	825	45.8%
Paris-Telephone	40	1,703	97.7%	185	3,164	94.5%
Paris & Seine-Post	2,233	485	17.8%	2,948	806	21.5% *
Paris-Ambulatory	1,955	-	0	2,838	-	0
Departments-Ambul.				647	-	0
Departments-Post, Telegraph, Telephone	5,408	3,851	41.6%	6,435	6,369	49.7%
Total	10,418	6,764	39.3%	14,028	11,164	44.3%

*The increase reflects the greater use of women in the Paris suburbs and not in Paris proper.

Source: Sembat, CDRCB, Exercise 1903 (Paris, 1902), pp. 194-96; Keratry, *Rapport présenté à la Commission extra-parlementaire des Postes et des Télégraphes* (Paris, 1911), pp. 315, 328.

vinces, were growing at a much faster rate than postal or telegraph services. Thus, between 1902 and 1911, the percentage of *dames employées* in Paris who worked in telephone services rose from 58 percent to 66 percent of the total number of women employed in the city. Telephone work became women's work par excellence, just as clerical and sorting work on the ambulatory railroad cars remained men's work. Almost equal numbers of men and women worked in telegraph services, but the two sexes as a rule remained physically segregated in separate rooms. Post office work proper employed men predominantly, and many *dames employées* in postal bureaus worked in mostly female groups with men supervisors. Before examining the extent to which such job segregation affected relationships between men and women employees after 1900, it is necessary to look more closely at the work and employment patterns of the *dames employées*.

Chapter Six:
Dames Employées:
Women's Work in the City

The year is 1900. She is twenty-two years old and it was her first train trip. After many hours she has finally arrived. Descending slowly from the wagon, the slight woman in the long, navy, fur-trimmed overcoat and large-brimmed hat struggles with her bulging carpetbag. As she moves along the busy *quai,* fears of what lie ahead mingle with thoughts of the family she has left behind. Home is a small town in the Dordogne, 450 kilometers to the south. There lives her mother, who, but for the need to stay with her younger son, would have accompanied her daughter, helped settle her in the city, and eased the transition. The novice *dame employée*'s first concern is to find a place to stay. She has the address of a small hotel not far from the station, and after a short trip on the omnibus she reaches her destination. There she meets several future colleagues, and that afternoon they set out together to look for more permanent lodgings. In the 6th Arrondissement they find a furnished room for rent: a narrow bed, one chair, a small table—one person and, *voilà,* the plank floor is covered. For that the unaffordable price of forty francs per month is asked. Immediately, the companions turn around and climb back down the narrow staircase. They next meet a colleague who has already been in Paris one month and who suggests they try her boarding house. She is unhappy there and wants to move, but she pays only fifty-five francs a month for both food and lodging. They visit the room shared by several boarders: beds half a meter wide with hardly a meter between. But there are no vacancies. Discouraged and far from reassured by the miserable lodgings they have viewed, the group returns to the hotel. Finally, after a week's searching, the *Dordognaise* finds an unfurnished attic room, a former maid's room, six flights up, for just over twenty francs a month; she will eat two small meals a day in a restaurant and from time to time, buy some bread, cheese, and fresh fruit to eat in her room.[1]

Distance from family, cramped living space, an inferior diet, a damp climate, the faster rhythm and anonymous faces of the metropolis—these were the immediate differences that struck many women who arrived in Paris around 1900 to work for the Postal Administration (or for what contemporaries were beginning more correctly to call the P.T.T., short for the merged postal, telegraph, and telephone services). While their postal brothers fresh from the provinces shared many of the same experiences, the transition was ruder for these young women, who had enjoyed greater parental and societal protection for most of their lives. Except for the women who roomed in boarding houses run by religious orders, the first generation of P.T.T. employees of provincial origins generally lived outside any kind of *in-loco parentis* arrangements. Of course, some women bid glad farewell to their hometowns and looked forward to their greater freedom in the city.[2] As a group *dames employées* escaped the community surveillance and social isolation which provoked so many complaints from *receveuses*. But, particularly in the beginning of their employment, material and psychological problems were usually so great that most provincials could not help but envy their Parisian peers who lived at home or the *dames employées* and *receveuses* who worked in their home departments or regions.

The provincial *dame employée* in Paris epitomized the modern twentieth-century female wage earner who lived apart from her family. But few women from the outset desired or were even conscious of this distinction. Indeed, in some regards, they continued to have one foot firmly planted in the nineteenth century. While feminists were still justified in applauding the expansion of employment opportunities for women, the *dames employées'* work hardly provided an example of the emancipation of women.

The typical *dame employée* appointed to Paris after 1900 began her employment in a telephone bureau, as did many women who began their careers in the provinces. Administrators and writers shunned the term "operator" in favor of the more genteel expression *"demoiselle du téléphone,"* which accurately reflected the employees' status before the war in the fledgling telephone service. (By 1912 there were still fewer than 300,000 telephone subscribers in all France.[3] The term "operator" did not enter into everyday use until the late 1920s, when, perhaps not coincidentally, automatic telephone services appeared. Yet, even before the inter-war period, the appellation *demoiselles* became more and more incongruent: The *demoiselles du téléphone* of Paris in the Belle Epoque worked in industrial-like settings that bore little resemblance to the first French telephone bureaus.

In 1885, six years after the telephone had made its appearance in France, the bureau on the rue Lafayette in Paris had one room with sixteen employees, one directress who supervised them, and one male inspector who oversaw the rudimentary equipment. Calls were infrequent enough that the *demoiselles,* fashionably attired in the tight-fitting, long, billowing dresses of the day, sat in chairs several feet away from the telephone equipment. When her line clacked, the *demoiselle* rose gracefully from her seat to answer the subscriber's call.[4] The largest bureau at the time, on the avenue de l'Opéra, had only thirty employees divided between two rooms. But work conditions changed dramatically in Paris as the number of subscribers grew in the 1890s. In the busiest central bureaus the addition of employees created cramped, unhealthy working conditions. Employees were required to be on their feet for long hours and some days to work for extended ten and a half hour shifts. The effects of such conditions on employees' health were readily apparent: the woman physician employed by the administration reported that one of ten employees was ill each day.[5]

The state considered a complete rebuilding of the Parisian telephone network essential for the development of services in France and began to realize its program of consolidation and expansion in the decade after 1889, when it had assumed total ownership and control of all telephone services. The opening of a large, central telephone bureau on the rue Gutenberg, behind the Hôtel des Postes in the commercial heart of Paris, marked the completion of the first phase of this plan. In addition to handling urban lines, the "Hôtel de Gutenberg" was the terminus for the more slowly developing international, inter-urban, and suburban lines. By 1905 the large-scale operation employed over 1,000 *dames employées* who worked in three daytime shifts, plus a small night work force of men. The other six bureaus in Paris had contingents of 100 to 300 employees each.[6]

In some respects, the construction of the Hôtel de Gutenberg marked an improvement in work conditions for telephone employees. The new buildings were more spacious and better lit, and while the employees still had to bend and stretch to hook up lines, they at least worked seated. The new equipment permitted a more efficient use of personnel and a shorter work day of seven hours. In exchange, however, the work pace was more intense;

employees now handled an average of 80 to 100 subscribers instead of the former 25. Special *"salons de repos"* had to be established so that workers could take short rest periods. What was worse, telephone services continued to suffer from inadequate personnel and equipment, namely, too few lines and defective materials.[7] As a result, the *demoiselles du téléphone* became the scapegoats for problems usually beyond their control.

Subscribers had quickly forgotten how difficult communications had been before the advent of the telephone. Easily frustrated by long delays and difficulties in obtaining connections, they focused their anger on the *demoiselles,* whom some accorded treatment little better than that they showed their domestic servants. Journalists and other writers helped sustain the subscribers' ire. "The telephones continue to function in a manner totally shameful for a city like Paris," commented one writer in *La Presse.* "In some bureaus it is necessary to wait twenty minutes to obtain the connection: the good *demoiselles* are more or less surly, and rarely obliging."[8] "All Paris amused itself in 1891 . . . at the productions of *La Demoiselle du Téléphone,"* an historian of French telephone services tells us. The burlesque play, which enjoyed a "wild success," portrayed the *demoiselles* as "wise little Parigots" (Parisians) who "cackle like hens" and listen in on the conversations.[9] A decade later the new hit was *Téléphoneries,* a comedy centered on the misadventures of an old man inadvertently thrown in with the female apprentices at the P.T.T.'s training school for telephone work.[10]

The attempts of more sympathetic writers to deflect the criticism heaped on the employees failed. Thus, *Salut Public* regretted that "we torment the *demoiselles du téléphone* like little children who torment flies because they do not cry out" and attributed to the "positivism of the age" the inability to pity what is unseen.[11] Séverine, one of the outstanding woman journalists of the day, concurred, describing the *demoiselles* romantically as "young, mostly pretty young women who have the instinct of elegance developed by their upbringing."[12]

But the public did not let up. The celebrated "Sylviac Affair" of 1904 set a Parisian actress against the *demoiselles.* Mlle Sylviac had grossly insulted an employee, and the administration decided to hold her up as an example by abrogating her use of the service and taking her to court on the criminal offense of insulting a civil servant. But the court chose in this instance, to deny the demoiselle the protection of civil servant status. Basking in the extensive press coverage, the

FIGURE 5. Training course for telephone employees (c. 1900). (Courtesy of Musée de la Poste)

FIGURE 6. Gutenberg Telephone Central, Paris, (c. 1900). (Courtesy of Musée de la Poste)

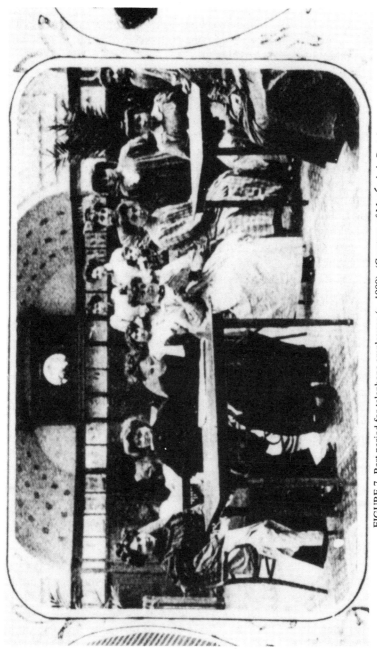

FIGURE 7. Rest period for telephone employees (c. 1900). (Courtesy of Musée de la Poste)

elegant Sylviac was vindicated, and at the constituent assembly of a new "League of Subscribers," one enthusiast ventured to proclaim her another Jeanne d'Arc.[13]

Discipline had always been strict in the telephone bureaus, and public pressure forced administrators to be even more severe. House rules closely resembled those of a girls' boarding school with women supervisors playing the role of sub-mistress.[14] All absences from the switchboard, including trips to the washroom, were strictly controlled. The paternalistic character of the discipline was fully revealed during the events of March 1909, when telephone employees joined the strike initiated by their colleagues in postal and telegraph services. One striking employee then confided to a reporter that the *demoiselles du téléphone* were treated like "little girls: reprimanded if they sat sideways instead of face front, given a bad mark for the slightest offense."[15] A form of punishment unique to telephone services was the denial of what normally would have been a half or full day of rest. This measure was self-defeating, as it served only to aggravate health problems caused by strains of the work.[16]

Telephone administrators themselves recognized the particular physical demands imposed on telephone workers. Ministerial archives show that the Director of Electrical Services lobbied strongly for a modification of recruitment and employee policies so that telephone workers be hired and dismissed according to different criteria than employees for other services. Most needed, in his view, were "girls endowed with a robust constitution, excellent health, perfect hearing, and a clear and well-pitched voice." He expressed dissatisfaction with the older, former *aides* of provincial origins who, he maintained, brought the "bad habits of the small bureau to the city."[17] But continuing to militate against a change in the recruitment of telephone employees was France's reliance, until 1919, on the cheap, flexible labor of *aides* and the need to place the *aides* as regular civil servants in telephone bureaus.

The important point here concerns the character of the employees' work. They basically performed specialized, physical tasks consisting of the repetition of simple motions. In the new centrals, where there were so-called "multiple switchboards," the employee responded to a customer when the lamp lit above the "jack"—socket—of the caller. She inserted one plug in this jack, pressed a key, and asked for the number to be called. If the desired line was free, she put the other plug into the connecting jack and pressed a key that rang the telephone bell of the person being called. Lights on the switchboard showed when the call was answered and when either person hung up.[18] The employee made dozens and, in some services, hundreds of such motions every day.[19] The training period was short. Knowledge of a foreign language was essential among the employees who worked on international lines (and who received a small monthly bonus), but generally, education, upbringing, and accent were secondary in importance to physical stamina, and writers had reason to criticize the excessively literary tone of the competitive entrance examination.[20] A growing medical literature documented the auditory problems and nervous illnesses associated with telephone work.[21] The public tended at once to trivialize the employees' work and exaggerate their power in controlling communications: Proust captured the mentality of subscribers of his generation when he immortalized the *demoiselles du téléphone* as mysterious muses who pulled at will the invisible strings of communication.[22] In fact, at the other end of the line, the employees' actions and their very movements were defined and limited by technology and managerial policies. Clearly, the *demoiselles du téléphone* did not find "emancipation" through work.

By comparison, the work of a post office clerk, as critics of the feminization policy pointed out, required more personal initiative and the performance of more varied tasks. The personal notebook kept by Mlle Camille Coquet, one of the first post office employees in Paris, shows well the character of the work. The notebook is crammed with information on calculating postal rates, filling out postal checks, depositing money in savings accounts, and figuring the cost of sending packages. There are even scrupulously neat drawings of the telegraph and telephone apparatuses, their mechanical parts, and functioning.[23] The variety of the tasks is one reason why experienced *aides* were usually assigned post office employment. Of course, this kind of petty bureaucratic work had its own form of tedium.[24] In addition, supervisors, the distinguished *receveur* or his chief clerk, constantly hovered about, and the demanding *"grincheux"* (grumpy) Parisians, often kept waiting in line, were not necessarily kinder in face-to-face contact than on the telephone. There was, moreover, a risk unique to this work. Employees were monetarily responsible for any error in cash transactions that could be traced to them. Insufficient numbers of employees and a poor organization of work continued to make time spent in the typically small, dusty, ill-lit post office an unpleasant experience for many a customer and employee.

If the opportunity arose, many women clerks, like their male col-

FIGURE 8. Paris post office (c. 1900). (Courtesy of Musée de la Poste)

FIGURE 9. Women operating sophisticated telegraph equipment at telegraph central in Paris (c. 1900). (Courtesy of Musée de la Poste)

leagues in Paris, preferred to work in the large telegraph central. Since the central was a kind of clearing-house for messages transmitted and received in Paris and between Paris and the departments or abroad, the great advantage of work in this setting was the absence of contact of any kind with the public. Traditionally there had always been a special esprit de corps at the central, which extended to the chief clerks and higher administrators and tempered hierarchical relationships. Further, telegraph employees, more than telephone workers, were able to set their own pace, which is why administrators offered incentives such as bonuses to encourage speed and accuracy in running the machines. Owing to these advantages, requests for transfers to the locale far outnumbered available openings. Only *dames employées* with exceptionally good connections could expect to receive an initial appointment to the central, and few even bothered to make the request. Since most, anxious to be placed as quickly as possible, took the advice to put themselves "at the disposition of the Administration."

Nonetheless, telegraph work in itself was almost as mechanical and monotonous as telephone work. Employees who operated the Morse apparatus used on all secondary lines pressed a key for longer or shorter intervals in combinations representing letters and symbols. These signals were then imprinted on paper at the receiving end of the line, where the employee transcribed the message into letters and words. The exceptional women who operated the Hughes telegraph used on major lines worked in teams of two: one employee transmitted the telegraph message by pressing letters on the keyboard, while the second employee checked the telegrams transmitted for errors, verified the number of words, noted the time of the transmission, and so forth. As a result of the frequent repetition of similar movements, some telegraphists developed what one physician, a Dr. Onimus, termed "telegraph cramp."[25]

Not only was individual autonomy limited in these work places: the employment also failed to provide the novice *dame employée* with real economic independence. In the decade from 1893 to 1903, the annual minimum income of women employed in postal and telegraph services in Paris was 1150 francs, a sum calculated by substracting the employee's share toward her pension (5 percent of the base salary) and adding the 200 franc cost of living allowance for Paris. Telephone employees in Paris earned 1450 francs annually; the difference reflected the one franc telephone employees received daily to defray meal costs, a tradition instituted by the private telephone companies and maintained by the state.[26] *Dames employées* residing in the provinces earned 1050 francs.

It was possible to survive on such an income, but only on the tightest budget providing for the bare minimum and with little leeway in the case of unforeseen expenses. The 100 franc raise legislators voted in 1904 was a mere token. It was extremely difficult for an individual to live in Paris on an income equivalent to three to four francs daily. Many women employees, just as men, lived in neighborhoods distant from the Paris center; most popular choices were the lower rent sections of Grenelle (15th), Vaugirard (15th), and Batignolles (17th).[27] Considering that the new *dame employée* earned the same base salary as had starting *receveuses*, who also received an allowance to defray the rent and lived in rural regions where the cost of living was lower, the material situation of the new generations of urban employees indicated a deterioration rather than an improvement in women's situation in the postal services.

The lingering emotional and material dependence of many female employees on their parents, and of families on their daughters, is concretely expressed in the letters *dames employées* or their parents wrote requesting a young woman's transfer closer to home. Thus, the schoolteaching father of one *dame employée* wrote: "This desire [to obtain a transfer] derives from the following reasons: [My daughter] is 660 kilometers from her family; her temperament, her nature, her feelings make her stay in Paris very hard; finally, she is obliged to rely too much on her father's salary."[28] "My request is motivated by the following reasons," explained a woman seeking a transfer from Paris back to Bordeaux. "My parents, who live in Bordeaux, need my help in raising my five-year old sister because my mother is in poor health . . . ; they also need my pecuniary aide which would be most efficacious if I lived with them at home."[29] "The climate of the Seine is very hard on her, especially in winter," another *dame employée*'s father implored before mentioning the importance to him and his wife of their only child's presence and support.[30]

At the turn of the century most women waited at least two to three years to obtain the transfer and usually appealed to departmental prefects and other intermediaries in their efforts. Over the long term, transfers of this kind became increasingly difficult as the number of employees grew as did the proportion of recruits from the less industrialized southwest. A vicious circle was set up whereby the places for new, younger employees in this region constantly decreased because of the seniority rights of older employees seeking to return to the region. A parliamentary report published in 1911 shows that Bordeaux and Toulouse ranked at the top of the cities requested by *dames employées* seeking transfers. The same report indicated that 56 percent of the women employees in telephone centrals in Paris and 54 percent of those in the telegraph central were of provincial origins; 42 percent of all women employed in these locales lived "at their own expense" rather than "with their family."[31] It is relevant to note that a recent study of P.T.T. employees from southern departments who are currently employed in Paris, suggests the continuing lack of integration of many provincials, men and women, into Parisian life.[32]

That the P.T.T. Administration also recognized the inadequacy of the *dames employées'* salaries and the problems of transition is reflected in the palliative measures established to provide better and reasonably priced food and lodging. In the late 1880s, the first cafeteria for employees in administrative offices had opened: for twelve sous (sixty centîmes) both men and women could obtain a full-course meal of soup, meat, salad, and coffee. Soon after a buffet-restaurant was installed in the postal savings bank offices. In the vicinity of the telegraph and telephone centrals certain restaurants, so-called *"midinettes,"* reserved special rooms for the *dames employées* who could buy partially subsidized meals for fifty centîmes. Cafeterias were then installed in the telegraph central and many of the telephone centrals, the innovations sometimes resulting from the demands of the employees themselves.[33] Finally, in 1903 the construction began of a six-story *"Maison des Dames,"* on the centrally located rue de Lille (7th), where it still stands and serves as housing for women from the provinces. The dormitory, the prototype of many present-day *foyers,* had 100 single bedrooms, a comfortable library, a salon, a garden, and a dining room which also served as a restaurant for non-resident employees. Anti-clerical sentiments helped foster the project as republicans wished to dissuade *dames employées* from lodging *chez les religieuses.*[34]

Some supporters of *"La Maison"* viewed the housing as a means of moral protection for young women away from home. The concern reflected the fact that a minority of women chose to ease their material situations by living with men outside the bonds of marriage. In Paris, like any other city, an unmarried *dame employée* who became pregnant and then failed to hide her condition was dismissed with no recourse. Though they may have shown more compassion toward their colleagues, most *dames employées* probably disapproved of such behavior, since before their admission to employment, the candidates had been more or less carefully screened to weed out those of "dubious morality."

In his novel, *Mademoiselle Téléphone* (1903), Paul Voucet portrayed one "fallen" *dame employée* as a lesson to all. Augustine was the daughter of provincial shopkeepers. At first she made ends meet in Paris only with the help of her father and by renting a room "so small that if the girls in her village had seen it, she would have blushed." Described as having a "weak character" and "superficial education," Augustine decided to set up housekeeping with a shop clerk who would "help [her] to live." The arrangement produced an unwanted pregnancy.

It is important to recall that, notwithstanding the rhetoric deploring the work of married women outside the home, *dames employées* were not obliged to leave the work force upon marriage. Despite the inferior status and wages of women in the P.T.T. relative to men, *dames employées,* like *receveuses,* enjoyed equally the full rights of civil servants. This situation contrasted sharply with the "marriage bar" that existed in state-run services in Germany, England, and Switzerland, as well as privately owned telephone services in the United States.[35] Nor were there any other policies designed to promote a turnover of employees. Administrators attempted twice before 1914 but failed to introduce a system of hiring telephone operators as *journalières* paid a daily wage and subject to dismissal. Critics argued that it was "inhumane" to dismiss women when they were too old to find other work. Instrumental in preventing the institution of such a system in 1910 was the same conservative, paternalistic Senate that would deny Frenchwomen the vote in 1919.[36]

What is more, an important measure was passed in 1903 which allowed *dames employées* a maternity leave of thirty-five days, over and above absences allowed for illness or personal reasons. This policy was one of the first of its kind in France, its passage owing much to the intense lobbying efforts of women employees in organized groups.[37] More *ad hoc* policies saw directors at the telegraph central in Paris permitting new mothers to nurse their babies at work, where a special room was set aside for this purpose, and the administration encouraging all locales, including telephone centrals, to adopt this policy.[38] All these measures, as well as the possibility for women to leave the work force to bear children then return, should be viewed in light of the climate of national opinion which decried the low French birthrate. But they do not appear to have been successful. It is doubtful that as a group women in the P.T.T. even reproduced themselves: they tended to bear only one or two children, and continued to have a high rate of celibacy.

In spite of their comparatively good situation, *dames employées* who were also wives and mothers continued to face difficulties beyond those of most single women. Employment away from the home, on split shifts, which were common in P.T.T. work, posed special problems. In the telegraph central in Paris, for example, employees worked alternate days in shifts that were, the first day, from seven to eleven in the morning and six to nine in the evening, then, the next day, from eleven to six. In the telephone bureaus, the shifts were seven in the morning to 12:15 in the afternoon and 7:15 to 9:15 in the evening, then the following day, from noon to 7:15.[39] These hours, so disruptive of domestic routines, helped reinforce ideological pronouncements which relegated women to the home. They also heightened women's own feelings of regret or ambivalence about working outside the home. Indeed, despite the existence of maternity leaves, the turnover rate was higher for *dames employées,* who were more likely to leave the work force after marriage, than had been true for women appointed *receveuses.* Illnesses also took a greater toll on women employed in urban settings, particularly in Paris where respiratory diseases like tuberculosis were common at the turn of the century.[40]

CAREER PATTERNS

As we have seen, women had been recruited expressly as *dames employées* to fill dead-end positions and were denied promotion to chief clerk rank, the entry grade for advancement to higher supervisory grades. This inferiority of opportunity for veteran employees meant that, over time, the disparity between the salaries of the two sexes widened. Of the approximately 18,000 *dames employées* and *receveuses* in the P.T.T. in 1909, well over half (60 percent) had entered the administration before 1900 and almost one of four (24 percent) before 1890. The *dame employée* who had entered in 1899 earned, with ten years' seniority, a fixed salary of 1500 francs, a 50 percent increase over her starting salary; her older colleague with twenty years' employment typically earned a flat salary of 2000 francs; and the doyenne of the group received, on the verge of retirement, 2200 francs, the maximum fixed salary for *dames employées*. *Receveuses* with equivalent tenures earned respectively 1400 francs, 1600 to 1800 francs, 1600 to 2200 francs. Their maximum salaries continued to depend on the importance of the bureaus they ran, but in all cases, their real incomes with special allowances added, usually surpassed that earned by *dames employées*. These figures show clearly that salaries rose most sharply for all women in the first twenty years of their employment, and that salaries then flattened out as employees reached the maximum. In comparison, the salaries of men generally rose more steeply throughout their careers. The typical man who entered the administration as a clerk in 1879 was earning, thirty years later, a maximum of 4500 francs in the chief clerk rank. The exceptional man promoted to higher administrative positions—about 10 percent of all clerks—earned more, in the range of 5000 francs and up, while at the other extreme, the minority of men never promoted out of the regular clerk ranks earned less—3300 to 3600 francs.[41]

In view of women's inferiority relative to men and special problems of women working outside the home, it is particularly significant that many *dames employées* still had long careers. Almost two-thirds (64 percent) of the women who began their P.T.T. employment as *dames employées* at the end of the century remained in the work force for more than twenty years. The comparable figure for male clerks was just slightly higher—75 percent.[42] In addition to job security and the incentives of raises and a retirement pension, long employment records also reflected the possibility of most older employees to assume jobs that were less physically demanding. Thus, while women were denied real promotional opportunities, they seldom remained throughout their careers in the same jobs they had filled as novices.

Of *dames employées* born in the provinces and who reached retirement in the 1920s and early 1930s, almost half (45 percent) eventually won appointment as *receveuses*. This position was filled mainly through internal recruitment after 1893. Both single and married women equally attained these appointments, so aspirations to manage provincial post offices cannot be attributed, as some writers suggested, solely to a woman's desire to work near her family in the home. The opportunity to work in one's home region as well as the potential for higher earnings and better living conditions were also important considerations. In addition, there was the attraction of being one's own boss. When S. de Lange left her position as a *dame employée* to become a *receveuse,* she missed the feeling of being able to leave her work behind her at the end of the day—"I was happy without knowing it," she wrote—but she gained something else in this exchange: she was no longer "simply one unit among many . . . the equivalent of a second-class soldier in the barracks."[43] She had lost one kind of freedom but gained another.

Another 16 percent of provincial-born employees became supervisors *(surveillantes)* in telephone or telegraph centrals where they earned supplementary wages of 400 to 600 francs. Still another 17 percent finished as office employees proper, some in the central ministry in Paris but most in the departmental offices of the postal savings bank. There they earned the same wages as *dames employées* in outside services but enjoyed a regular, nine-to-five work day and escaped working Sundays and holidays. In contrast, among Parisian retirees, a much smaller proportion (17 percent) became *receveuses,* while 43 percent attained the position of supervisor, and 22 percent entered office work.

Though none of these positions had either the higher wages or status associated with male promotional slots, the relative mobility women experienced was significant, compared both to their entry level positions and to the popular class origins of many of the women. Besides reflecting a generational difference, the differences in status were clear between a *receveuse* and her subordinate *aide* or between a telephone supervisor and an operator. Photographs of telephone centrals show the more distinguished demeanor and dress of the supervisors compared to the switchboard workers. Young women at once resented the authority of their immediate female supervisors and aspired to step into their shoes.

A minority of women who remained employed as ordinary *dames employées* throughout their careers were also better situated at the end of their employment than at the beginning. In telephone services in Paris, for example, older women often left the switchboard to work as record keepers *(employées aux écritures),* at tables which lined the center of the aisles between operators. Generally, women employees adopted personal strategies from the outset of their employment to minimize the most unpleasant aspects of their work. Judging from employee records, the Gutenberg central was one of the least desirable places to work, and women seldom remained there for any length of time. Either they obtained a transfer to the provinces, where work conditions were usually more relaxed, changed to a smaller bureau in Paris, or if they had the proper training, switched to postal or telegraph services (though the ensuing loss of the special meal allowance given Parisian telephone employees reduced the attraction of the latter). Relative satisfaction in a particular bureau also depended in part on the manager, who had considerable freedom in setting the tone of the work place and employee policies. Unpopular bosses like the Gutenberg's principal engineer, Bouchard, were the targets of verbal abuse during periods of open conflict, as during the strike of 1909. In normal times, a "bad" administrator could provoke an employee to seek a transfer to another bureau.[44]

The paperwork involved in all these transfers was staggering, no less than the problem of personnel instability, about which administrators constantly complained. That the practices still persisted reflected several factors: the dynamic of old bureaucratic traditions, paternalism, and administrators' own desires to have the youngest and most physically fit employees in the most fatiguing positions. There was also the need to maintain, at no apparent cost, a minimal level of employee morale essential to the smooth running of the services. Finally, there was the chronic problem of having to free up entry level positions for the *aides* pushing from below for civil service appointments.

Once having grasped the character of the *dame employée*'s work and the limited structure of opportunity, writers like Camille Rouyer, author of *La Femme dans l'Administration* (1900), were forced to qualify their generally positive assessments of the employment of women in the civil service. But by the same token, a more judicious view of women's employment histories would have provoked some refinement in the portrait of the exploited female wage earner drawn for polemical purposes by politicians like deputy Groussier, who facilely and indiscriminately lumped together all women who worked for wages. The P.T.T. itself offered concrete examples of the significant differences in status, material situation, and autonomy among female wage earners at the turn of the century, as can be seen by comparing the *dame employée* and *receveuse,* the novice *dame employée* and the veteran.

An even more telling comparison is that between the *dame employée* and *aide*. The *aide* was in every sense dependent on the manager of the post office where she worked. In the typical situation where the *aide* lodged with the *receveuse,* the latter could call on her at will for assistance, remunerate her as she wished (and the market would bear), and dismiss her whenever she felt just cause. If the *aide* failed to work because of illness, she certainly did not receive full pay up to three months' absence, as did *dames employées,* nor did she enjoy the *dame employée*'s right to a two weeks' paid vacation. Totally lacking the protection granted the *dame employée* as a full civil servant, the *aide* depended totally on the good will of the post office manager. Under these circumstances, the situation of the *aide* varied from one post office to the next, but more than one observer related her position to that of the domestic servant. Given the choice, *receveuses* themselves often preferred *aides* to regularly salaried employees because *aides* were more "docile." And the administration itself avoided placing *aides* in secondary bureaus in more urban locales since they knew *aides* quickly became aware of the disparity between their lot and the relative freedom and material well-being of the *dames employées.*[45] Indeed, this was the same lens through which many *dames employées,* former *aides,* themselves viewed their position, at least in the beginning.

Moreover, *dames employées* who had grown up in Paris or other large cities were well aware of the less enviable position of their sisters and neighbors who worked in shops or in the garment trades. There, they knew, seasonal unemployment and dismissals were commonplace and remuneration generally dependent on the number of hours worked or of pieces sewn.

It was the very exceptional conditions of employment and long tenures that help explain why many women became involved in P.T.T. employee associations permitted by the law of 1901, while over the same period the participation of female wage earners in industrial unions remained markedly low. Most women joined the *Association générale des Agents* founded by their male colleagues. But a small group of highly educated *dames employées,* feminists who were particularly frustrated by their inferior position relative to men in the P.T.T., would strike out on their own path of collective actions.

Chapter Seven:
The P.T.T. Family:
In Harmony and Discord

Our administration is the one where the greatest camaraderie exists and where the personnel show the greatest affection for their supervisors . . . Our colleagues . . . went in a body to the home of their director to offer him their congratulations on the occasion of his recent investiture [into the Legion of Honor] . . . This family party at which all ranks of the hierarchy . . . were represented was marked by the most sincere cordiality.[1]

This social report appeared in *Le Journal des Postes* next to more serious columns which presented the complaints and demands of employees. This report was from Digne (Gap) in 1885, but hundreds of similar reports appeared before and after the turn of the century. Postal employees of all ranks celebrated together the significant events that marked their lives: the award of a distinguished state honor, as above, or more commonly, a promotion or retirement. And at times of illness or death, employees of the administration were present to offer their condolences and assistance. Despite the steady growth of the P.T.T. family after 1900, the sense of camaraderie and membership in a group remained strong.

The incorporation of women into the urban P.T.T. work force added a new dimension to the family body. Some social events remained all-men affairs where the mixing of sexes was considered "incorrect". No women appeared, for example, at the *"punch d'adieu"* offered a retiring *receveur* at the Café de Paris in Bourg (Ain); they joined in the spirit of the occasion, instead, by presenting a "beautiful green plant" to the *receveur*'s wife.[2] Just as often, however, women employees participated in the so-called *fêtes de famille,* assuming the role in some instances of dutiful daughters. At the retirement of the *receveur* at Valence (Drôme), the *dame employée* who presented the bouquet to his wife expressed her regrets at the departure of the *receveur* who was "for [them] all and especially for the *dames employées* . . . a veritable family father."[3] As mutual aid societies institutionalized some social functions after 1900, and their leaders sought women's enrollment, women employees appeared publicly more and more, even at evening meetings. "Ah, how you have changed us, mesdames, from these interminable after-dinners 'among men'" were the welcoming remarks of the departmental director of Gironde at one party of an *amicale* in Bordeaux, where around thirty *dames* "displayed their charming outfits, as simple as they were tasteful."[4] Dances and cultural events also brought men and women together. The telegraph central in Paris, for example, frequently sponsored musical concerts and recitations.[5] At the Paris Exposition of 1900, contingents of men and women P.T.T. employees from all over France voyaged to the capital, where they attended *en masse* a comic opera gala, toured Versailles, and visited the monuments of Paris. They danced into the wee hours of the morning, joined by the "intrepid *demoiselles*" from the Gutenberg and Villette telephone bureaus who were "held closely by [members of] the delegation from Marseille."[6]

Affective ties to those who shared the same work place, social relations in leisure hours, and marital alliances between men and women employees all worked to diminish hostilities toward women's employment on the part of men and resentment at their inferior status in the administrative hierarchy on women's part. Though distinctive and separate forms of female socializing and male camaraderie developed, women nonetheless shared the esprit de corps that bound P.T.T. employees together across gender, seniority, rank, and work place. Indeed, in terms of their social identities, women stood closer to men clerks and men in other male white-collar grades *(agents)* than did the latter to mail carriers and men in other lower administrative ranks *(sous-agents).* The public controversy surrounding the feminization policy notwithstanding, then, it is not surprising that after 1900, most men and women would collaborate in collective actions aimed to further administrative reforms or to protest the degradation of their material situation. The segregation of women into a separate female grade and their concentration in telephone services sometimes slowed, but did not stop, collaboration between the sexes.

Thus, though no women were among the founders of the *Association générale des Agents des P.T.T.* (A.G.), women had a place in the employee organization virtually from the beginning. At the first general assembly in 1901, one male delegate caused a minor uproar when he stated that ''we do not have to bother about the *dames* since they are not part of our association,'' a comment which was incorrect, since some women were in fact already members. But the official reception was more generous; the report of the assembly mentioned that ''several *dames,* ravishingly dressed, filled the first rows of the audience.''[7] In 1902, two of twenty-seven members of the *conseil d'administration,* the governing body of the A.G., were women. Their presence provoked the staunchest opponents of the feminization policy to raise anew their anti-women banners. ''This new element will bring no capabilities and it is a purely moral satisfaction which is being offered out colleagues of the weaker sex,'' commented the editor of *L'Union des P.T.T.* ''They would be just as well if not better off, defended by leaders of the opposite sex.''[8] But the leadership of the association clearly realized the need to include women in the membership and leadership.

The A.G.'s decision to include women reflected the realization that the organization's strength lay in numbers. In the provincial departments where the concentration of clerks was usually sparse, the recruitment of *dames employées* as well as *receveuses* helped to establish the quota needed for the formation of local departmental groups. Efforts to organize the telephone and telegraph employees in Paris also began in earnest. By the end of 1902, there were groups organized at Gutenberg and several other centrals. Helping to assuage the *dames employées'* fears of reprisals were the encouragement offered by a personal representative of the director of telephone services and the reassurances of Minister Millerand. In fact, the growth of the A.G. as a whole was encouraged by the government, which hoped, in permitting the formation of employee associations, to solidify the support of its civil servants in the wake of the Dreyfus Affair (1894-1899).[9] By 1903, the association had 16,000 members, organized in eighty departments.

Women themselves also helped convince the association of the usefulness of their participation and the importance of their demands. In 1900, after an unfruitful meeting with the Director of Personnel in Paris, three women employees decided to establish a

journal dedicated to defending the particular interests of female personnel. In July 1900, a committee composed of six *dames employées*
and three *receveuses* put out the first issue of the monthly, *L'Union
des Dames de la Poste.* The lack of attention paid female employees
in the "masculine journals" and the same journals' efforts "for
many years . . . to combat without respite the feminist movement
[that is, the feminization policy]" nourished the enterprise. As one
reporter wrote, there had existed no organ in the 1890s "to take up
the gauntlet in favor of the misfortunate female employees sometimes
so odiously   slandered."[10] With some justification, *L'Union des
Dames'* editors asserted that it was a mark of their success that the
A.G. had "opened wide its doors to the female employees, recog-
nize[d] their demands as legitimate, and present[ed] them in high
places."[11] In 1902 and 1903 the journal adopted the position that it
was necessary "to rally frankly and work in concert" with the A.G.
but that *Union's* "independent" action was "indispensable" in promoting the women employees' interests in an organization where
men far outnumbered women. Hence the editors of *L'Union des
Dames* published reports of A.G. activities and encouraged their
readers to become members, while they simultaneously acted as
watchdogs over its pronouncements and refused to "go over" to
A.G.'s official organ, *Le Professionnel.* [12]

L'Union des Dames* was clearly an undertaking animated by
reciprocal contacts between women P.T.T. employees and feminist
groups in Paris. Marguerite Durand, the most eminent feminist in
France around 1900, featured articles on women in the P.T.T. in
her daily, *La Fronde,* and she herself inquired into the conditions of
advancement for women in the services.[13] During 1903 Renée Ram-
baud, a contributor to *La Fronde,* served as editor-in-chief of
L'Union des Dames; on its pages she echoed the sentiments Julie
Daubié had expressed forty years earlier in asserting that postal
employment was potentially an excellent career for women, if only
wages and promotional opportunities were better.[14] Maria Martin's
Le Journal des Femmes, another leading feminist periodical, continued as in the 1890s to maintain ties to the women employees,
sometimes running excerpts from *L'Union des Dames.* [15]

Though the editors of *L'Union des Dames* were conscious of the
need to avoid offending their more conservative readers and keep to
the defense of professional interests, they occasionally published articles on subjects such as the reform of the civil code and women's

suffrage.[16] In this way they helped carry on the work of some of their subscribers, among whom must have figured Mlle Nicodse, *receveuse* at Monbenoît, who lectured members of her provincial community on the "respect owed woman"; her presentation included an unflattering portrait of the "rustic *foyer*" where the wife was regarded as "a servant . . . held to the feudal custom denying her a place at the table of the *seigneur* during family gatherings" and also an energetic pronouncement in favor of women's suffrage and of "a radical rewriting of the [Civil] Code in the direction of veritable equality."[17] Another subscriber had to have been postal employee Renee Mortier, who had married "out of love" a man with whom she had had a child and who, with Hubertine Auclert, presented her candidacy in the 11th Arrondissement of Paris in the 1910 legislative elections.[18]

One of the collaborators in founding *L'Union des Dames,* Mme Chambin, was one of the first two women elected to the A.G.'s *conseil d'administration.* A Parisian and employee at the telegraph central, she was a *déclassée* whose views and privileged upbringing are indicative of those of many women supporters of *L'Union.* Highly educated and articulate, Chambin was described by one male interviewer as a pretty woman whose sexual identity "one quickly forgot the moment she spoke, choosing her words with a mathematical precision more than one man could envy."[19] She espoused a "practical feminism" which aimed to "inculcate her companions with concrete ideas of solidarity" and to ameliorate women's situation within the administration. She was the moving force behind the A.G.'s demand for maternity leave for women employees, a successful effort the importance of which had required convincing some recalcitrant male colleagues.[20] At the general assembly of the A.G. in 1902, she was an outspoken defender of women's abilities and rights, as she highlighted the "disproportion" that existed between the professional knowledge required of the *dame employée,* her obligations of service, her responsibility—all equal to those of clerks—and "the derisory sum" she received for a starting salary. Chambin deserved some credit for the assembly's placing a raise in the minimum salary of *dames employées* as a first priority among all its demands.[21]

While maintaining her membership in the A.G., Mme Chambin formed a separate committee to seek salary raises for women employees. The committee's work consisted of a detailed, sixty-eight-page document distributed to the press and parliament in 1903. The preface of the *Mémoire* read:

> At the moment when all corporations are forming *syndicats* and associations to defend their just claims, women are forced to raise their voices, in order that they not be forgotten or neglected . . .
>
> Modern society has granted woman the right to work and to earn her living. It is necessary to give her this right completely and without the least restriction. That is to say, her labor must be remunerated just as that of man . . . she should not be obliged to furnish double the work for an inferior salary.[22]

Documenting the low salaries of women in the P.T.T., the committee then cited and refuted, point by point, the arguments regarding women's inferior abilities that Millerand (mentioned by name) and others had used to oppose the feminization policy:

> Every day . . . in the afternoon, one sees *dames* replacing their male colleagues, either at the postal counter or the [telegraph] apparatus. They will do exactly the same work, alternating one sex for the other over months and years . . . We will note in passing that this weakness and feminine inferiority that are constantly used as conclusive arguments each time we demand an equitable remuneration for our work, hinders in no way the excessive demands laced on *dames* in . . . telephone services.[23]

The combined work of the A.G. and *L'Union des Dames* helped to attract new women members to the association. At the third general assembly in May 1903, there were seventeen women among the 187 voting delegates. Though the number of women was much smaller than men and all but three of the women delegates were Parisians, the showing was a considerable improvement over the previous year, when only three women, all from the telegraph central, had appeared as delegates. For the first time, telephone employees were well represented, with six delegates from the Gutenberg central and three representatives from other bureaus in Paris.[24] With the growth in female membership, women outside the *L'Union des Dames* assumed positions of leadership in the A.G. At the 1903 assembly one of these women, Mlle Kuntz, who was an employee in the central administration, gave the principal address concerning women and the A.G. Her conciliatory, deferential words received loud applause. More representative of the women members' mentality than the feminist Chambin, Kuntz is worth quoting at length:

> Among the new formations of groups, we greet . . . with the greatest joy those of *dames*. They have shown us proof of energy and solidarity of union which augurs well . . . They have set an example of many men. We have met in these feminine groups women of elite [origins] animated by a veritable democratic spirit . . .
>
> . . . Unfortunately, there are still too many of our colleagues who do not understand the necessity of this grouping for the defense of interests; this will come. Their social education will grow little by little . . . Others are sceptical, believing that the Association works above all for the interests of men; you will help to prove them wrong by aiding us to bring to fruition our demands . . . We do not want to know, we new arrivals, if it was necessary to conquer the opinionated resistance of certain comrades poorly disposed towards the *dames;* we come to work together for the amelioration of the condition of all, persuaded that we will find in you . . . a spirit of fraternity and solidarity.
>
> . . . We count on you, dear comrades, to aid us with your experience, like older brothers have to do for the youngest [children] still lacking in experience . . . [25]

The absence of Chambin at the assembly reflected the already fragile relationship of the feminists to the association; the former rejected the role of younger sisters and refused to let bygones be bygones. Total rupture followed an important procedural change, voted at the same assembly, which forbade the existence of any separate group organized by administrative rank within the A.G. The argument that such groups threatened the unity and strength of the association had triumphed over the contending position that such groups were natural in view of the range of interests represented by the association and ought to be accommodated under its umbrella.[26] In October 1903 the *conseil d'administration* expelled Mme Chambin and leaders of other "dissident" groups, who subsequently formed their own associations.[27] Mme Chambin's new *Association des Dames Employées* first met in November of the same year.[28]

Between 1903 and 1909 the A.G. never regained its former strength as its membership hovered between roughly twelve and thirteen thousand.[29] Nonetheless, the association remained by far the strongest organization of white-collar employees in the P.T.T. and the only one that represented all services and administrative grades. In September 1905 the A.G. was capable of rallying 5,000 employees in Paris, men and women, to discuss remedies to a "postal crisis", which occurred when the seasonal increase in the use of P.T.T. services by summer vacationers aggravated existing personnel shortages, produced delays in mail deliveries and telegraph transmissions, and brought longer work days and heavier work loads.[30] A year later the association drew 3,000 employees to a meeting which addressed a demand for the six-day work week, just granted in law to workers in private industry but not public services.[31]

Though the A.G. lost some highly articulate women leaders to the *Association des Dames Employées,* it lost few of its female members. After 1904 the A.G. published no detailed statistics on its membership, making difficult an exact determination of the women within its fold. But in that year, the A.G. still included 1,804 *dames employées* and at least 1,000 *receveuses* among its reduced total membership of 11,673.[32] Women continued to serve on the *conseil d'administration,* usually taking four or five of some thirty seats. At every general assembly between 1904 and 1909, there were always nine or ten women delegates, most of them from Paris telephone centrals. A new leading spokeswoman emerged in Thérèse Pech, an employee in the telegraph central, where her husband, himself a militant in the A.G., also worked. Indefatigable, Mme Pech sometimes traveled outside Paris in efforts to recruit new members into the association. In 1906 the A.G. elected her to the position of adjoint-secretary of the *conseil d'administration,* the fourth highest office in the organization and the highest held by a woman before the war.[33]

Pech sought to reduce the frictions caused by the competing demands of clerks and *dames employées,* and toward this end, towed the A.G. line on salary questions. After 1903 the association decided to link the demand for raises in women's salaries to men's: any raise in clerks' salaries would require a raise for *dames employées,* the latters' salary to be maintained at the proportion of two-thirds of the clerks'. This tactic, which implied acceptance of the administration's rationale that three women did the work of two men, met with some success. In 1905 the legislature raised the maximum salary of *dames employées* to 2000 francs and again, in 1907, to 2200 francs, closely trailing the increase in clerks' maximum salary to 3300 francs.[34] However, women continued to have no access to the higher paying chief clerk and supervisory ranks, an issue the A.G. carefully sidestepped.

Despite the intense polemical battles waged by the A.G. and the *Association des Dames Employées,* the latter never constituted serious competition. At its height, membership in the all-women association failed to surpass four or five hundred. The splinter group clearly lacked the financial resources of the A.G. as well as the support the A.G. received among politicians. In addition, however democratic, Chambin and her colleagues found it hard to shed the taint of their relatively privileged upbringings, which showed immediately in the quality of the prose that set *L'Union des Dames* apart from all other employee journals. And their strong-minded feminism repelled socially conservative women as well as men. Many of their specific demands were far ahead of their time, for instance, the right for women to take the same entrance examination as men or to have access to higher grades. But they were bound to appeal to the best-educated, more middle-class women, who were the most qualified to step into higher positions and who needed most to develop a positive image of their employment, as a source of pride and independence, rather than simply a means of living.

By late 1906 *L'Union des Dames* had all but ceased reporting the *Association des Dames Employées'* activities, and the journal itself folded in 1908 for lack of support. Writers for *L'Union* had expressed growing disillusionment with how little they had advanced toward "equal salary for equal work" and described as "lip service" the support some legislators had given the demand.[35] One columnist wrote bitterly in early 1908:

> Why are women always neglected? Is it because they are not electors? Is it a consequence of a prejudice of bygone times? . . . the reign of equality is still not close to opening, despite all the fine words of our most ardent orators who seem to dispense all their energy in speeches, who think it suffices to

talk about a reform or formulate a platonic vow . . . for their
intentions to become fact . . . Alas! Messieurs, rhetors, between speech and action, there is an abyss . . : And you know
it well, babblers![36]

At least some of the feminists brought their anger back over to the
A.G.; by late 1908 one columnist from *L'Union des Dames* was
writing for the A.G.'s *Le Professionnel*.[37]
     The conflicts between the A.G. and the *Association des Dames
Employées* did not help to further the interest of women employees
in joining any association. Still, sectarian battles alone fail to explain
the lower rate for women's membership in associations relative to
men's. Even in Paris, where association activities were centered and
the concentration of employees facilitated their organization, one-
half to three-fourths of all *dames employées* never joined any
association in the first decade of the twentieth century. In comparison, the clerk who had joined an association was much
more typical than the clerk who had not, both in Paris and the provinces. Nor was the higher turnover rate of women sufficient cause
for such a difference; as we saw in the last chapter, most women had
long employment histories. While the long careers of many women
favored a relatively high participation compared to women in most
other occupations, many of the same factors traditionally cited as
hindering women's organization were operating in this setting as
well.
     Writers for *L'Union des Dames* suggested several causes of
women's indifference, including a "spirit of egoism" and reactionary ideas inculcated by the Church. Vanity also entered in:
"Many employees want to play a bourgeois role, to ape affluence
and disguise a too real poverty under the false appearance of well-
being," deplored Lucie de Villeneuve, lead columnist for the journal. She continued, explaining that she had received letters from
"colleagues who complain[ed] that the journal wound[ed] their
pride in airing publicly their misery." But most frequently cited was
the fact that many women in the P.T.T., as in other sectors, seemed
to regard their employment as transitory, until marriage (even if
they never realized such hopes), or their salaries as only a supple-
ment to their husbands' incomes.[38] The reality of low salaries and
dominant cultural attitudes which viewed the husband as chief
breadwinner could only have sustained such beliefs. Demonstrating
the limits on divergent beliefs in this period, even feminist postal

employees ventured to state that there was no "more beautiful role for us than that of wife and mother," even though in practice some had been unable to fulfill this "mission of woman."[39]

THE STRIKE OF 1909

Nonetheless, even many women previously indifferent to collective actions joined their colleagues in the strike of 1909, as the need to defend the common interests of the P.T.T. family temporarily overshadowed the conflicting demands of its members. White-collar *agents* in the lead, thousands of P.T.T. employees stopped working in the first national strike of civil servants in France. At the height of the strike, on 17 March 1909, Paris was cut off from the rest of France and the world. Hundreds of postal sacks piled up in railroad stations and post offices, thousands of telegrams sat waiting to be sent, all telephones were mute, business at the Bourse came to a standstill, and some frantic financiers left the capital to install themselves temporarily in Brussels.[40] Without the participation of women, the strike could never have come off, since women could have kept telegraph and telephone, if not postal services running. The fervency of the *dames employées* attracted particular public attention, and the presence of many women among the strikers helped legitimize the postal employees' grievances among large segments of the public.

General interpretations of the famous strike have focused on its significance in the broadening of the realm of labor strife to include new social strata outside the working classes proper, and on its origins in the proletarianization of the P.T.T. work force. It is certainly true that the physical labor involved in many work tasks, relatively low wages, and limited mobility had worked to enlarge the base of recruitment for women as well as men. Raises in P.T.T. employees' wages had failed to offset the rise in the cost of living in Paris and many other cities after the turn of the century.[41] Further, though the expansion of personnel appeared to keep up with the steady rise in communicatons after the 1905 crisis and the accompanying public outcry, work loads often remained high, and workers' rising expectations for shorter work weeks failed to be met.[42] If "proletarianization" is meant to imply increasing recruitment from the urban working class, however, the expression is misleading. The continuing trend instead was toward the recruitment of ever increasing numbers of men and women from rural milieus. Over a third (35.3 percent) of the women and nearly half (46.2 percent) of the men admitted in 1909-1910 came from southwestern France, the figures for both sexes significantly higher than two decades earlier.[43]

Particular problems in the recruitment of women had showed up first in the hiring of *aides.* In 1905, P.T.T. directors in twenty-eight departments signaled problems in finding *aides;* on the whole, the departments least affected were those in the less-industrialized Southwest and Center. Cited as causing the recruitment difficulties were insufficient remuneration, uncertainty concerning the future, the disproportion between the number of candidates for *dame employée* positions and the number of openings, and more advantageous jobs elsewhere. After the passage of the 1904 law forbidding teaching by religious orders and the expansion of jobs for female lay teachers, *aides* with diplomas began to emigrate into teaching; others without degrees began to seek jobs in commerce and industry.[44]

The immediate sources of discontent that triggered the strike in 1909 bore strong parallels to the cause of employee agitation two decades earlier: slowed advancement, the unresponsiveness of the administration and legislature to employees' protests, the repression of the most militant agitators, and the total loss of employees' confidence in their head. An appointee of the Clemenceau ministry constituted on 24 October 1906, the hard-nosed Julien Simyan, faithfully practiced the strong-arm tactics that characterized Clemenceau's approach to labor conflicts. By selectively slowing certain employees' advancement Simyan attempted to cut expenses, an understandable goal given the decline in net P.T.T. revenues after the lowering of postal rates in 1906 and the cyclical economic crisis of 1906-1907.[45] But his attempt to divide P.T.T. employees backfired dismally; Simyan underestimated the family loyalty and dislike of favoritism, which inevitably surfaced and won employees the support of many of their hierarchical superiors against the interloping political appointee. While the feminization policy had served earlier to ease sources of employee discontent, the new measures introduced by Simyan struck at the interests of all employees, including the very women brought into the work force in the 1890s.

Mobilization of women was easiest at the one place where they were concentrated in large numbers and where many men also worked: the telegraph central in Paris. The central had always been an important center for employee agitation, and owing to the bureau's proximity to central administration offices, demonstrations directed at Simyan frequently overflowed into the central's courtyard. Willingly or not, women, like men, were caught up in the struggle played out between the militants and the forces of order, that is, Simyan and the police. Thus, when Simyan and the chief of police, Lépine, entered the central on 15 March to expel a group of militants which included some women, the two men hurled epithets, effectively calling the latter whores *(salopes, filles)*. With these words, the intruders destroyed the illusion that the working women were "ladies."[46]

All the *dames employées* and their male protectors were outraged. The next day women helped disrupt the normal flow of telegraph communications; one uniquely female tactic consisted of sticking hatpins into the telegraph apparatuses to produce short circuits.[47] Equally important, the incident received wide press coverage. Recapturing the "telegraph revolt" for its curious readers, *L'Illustration* featured a full, front page drawing of one *dame employée*'s confrontation with Simyan and Lépine. In the background one clerk may be seen supporting another *dame employée* who had fainted.[48] The A.G. exploited the occasion to the utmost, and the insults helped rally almost overnight women employees in telephone centrals and some small post offices throughout the city.[49] The women's support was doubly impressive in view of Clemenceau's resolve to break the strike with army troops and reserves and by threatening to dismiss all participants.[50] Aiding the strikers in Paris were the participation or declarations of support from men and women employees in the provinces.[51]

At the height of the walkout, the strike headquarters for telephone employees at the Café Marengo on the rue St. Honoré were packed. When 250 to 300 employees from one shift at the Gutenberg arrived *en masse,* "onlookers and employees from the Louvre who had gone into the café to eat regarded them with intrigue," it was reported. Wrote *Le Matin* of the *demoiselles du téléphone:*

> If [the public] were in these rooms where the *[demoiselles]* exhale the bitterness of their hearts, if it could come to the Café Marengo where enthusiastically, passionately, they recount their sorrows, their rancors, their hopes of a better future, it would understand the excitement a feminine presence adds to the will of men . . . [52]

If the Simyan insults had touched off the telephone employees' "fever," (a word the press used constantly to describe the women's state of mind), perhaps it was because for them, more than was true for any other group, the strike was truly a moment of liberation, a brief respite from the particularly strict discipline imposed on them. Moreover, in publicly asserting their identity as workers, they were also challenging social attitudes identifying women primarily with domestic activities. And at least momentarily the employees themselves were able to forget their other, familial roles as they participated in a new kind of social experience.

At the moment when almost all P.T.T. employees in Paris were united in common action, one telephone employee, Mme Raspaud declared: "There is no longer a masculine proletariat and a feminine proletariat. There are only workers who suffer and bestir themselves."[53] The indomitable feminist Hubertine Auclert may have agreed with that sentiment as she praised the strikers' courage on the pages of *L'Egalitaire*. But the less socially minded, conservative feminists of *Le Conseil des Femmes* took issue with this point of view and did little to advance the cause of feminism among P.T.T. employees when it sought to have women fill the places of all strikers dismissed for their militancy.[54]

The strike was partially successful: Clemenceau withdrew the disputed measure regarding advancement, and Simyan was gone after 23 July 1909, when the Clemenceau ministry was dissolved. After the strike, however, underlying conflicts between women and men remained. At the 1913 general assembly of the A.G., one male delegate stated unequivocally that "an antagonism in fact exists between the female personnel and masculine personnel." He continued:

> This is a cause of weakness for our Association. We have to look at [this antagonism] head on and seek its remedy . . . .
>
> In suggestive fashion, I will expose the thesis of integral feminism . . . . [Men] say: Women at the present time are competition for us because they work for less . . . [A voice interrupted: it's not our fault!]
>
> How can we rid ourselves of this competition? The only way is to demand that the conditions of work for women be exactly the same as for men: that is, that one asks of women the same abilities and guarantees, but in return, they be offered access to the same jobs, the same moral and material situation.[55]

FIGURE 10. Men and women entering strike meeting, 1909. (Courtesy of Musée de la Poste)

This was an important admission, inconceivable a decade earlier. There is no doubt that women's employment with men as colleagues, their membership in the A.G., and the solidarity women employees showed in 1909, won them respect from most men over time. Still, it is also apparent that the enlightened male delegate who called for an "integral feminism" was voicing a minority opinion. The discussion at the 1913 meeting and others before the war revealed that many men continued to feel threatened by women and particularly objected to the idea of women supervisors. Other men, basing their position on the false assumption that women's cheapness alone promoted women's employment, argued sophistically that on the day women became their equals, the administration would no longer recruit them.[56] In effect, although the interests of the male clerks and male administrators remained far apart, the clerks continued to collude in shaping the limited contours of women's place in the administration.

Conclusion

Women who retired in 1914 left an administration that bore little resemblance to the separate postal and telegraph services some had entered on the eve of the merger in 1877, the year women first appeared as telegraph clerks in Paris. With the enormous expansion in the volume of telegraph and postal communications and the emergence of the telephone, the number of women employees had multiplied. However, this study has shown nothing, if not the fallacy of drawing from sheer numbers facile conclusions about the significance of the change for women.

On the one hand, the growth in the number of women working in the P.T.T. closely coincided with adverse changes in the character of their work. The kinds of postal, telegraph, and telephone jobs that *dames employées* as a group filled on the eve of the first world war required fewer skills, demanded less responsibility, and conferred less social prestige than the work some women had performed a century earlier as post office managers. On the eve of the war, the *receveuses des postes* remained somewhat exceptional among female employees in the P.T.T. Their work continued to require a range of knowledge, experience, and responsibilities (indeed the latter had grown since the merger), and the position usually retained a fair, albeit diminished, hold on the public's respect.

Over the long term, the steady growth in the number of female employees to fill more menial jobs was mirrored in the changing backgrounds of the recruits. By 1914 *dames employées* as a group were drawn from lower social backgrounds and were more likely to come from the less industrialized regions of France than the precious few women who pioneered working in urban settings in the late 1870s and 1880s. More often than not, women had first entered postal employment as lowly *aides* in smaller post offices. Receding further in time, many of that small number of privileged women of bourgeois and aristocratic origins who filled postal positions in the late eighteenth century very likely would have shunned postal employment in its early twentieth-century form.

Although some feminists had worked hard to promote women's

employment in the postal services, the increase in the number of women employed reflected no major change in attitudes toward women. The feminists' own disappointment showed in their evaluations of the position of the women employees. Patriarchal beliefs and power remained entrenched in the administration, just as in wider French society. Male employees had found effective support in their resistance to the perceived competition from women when they opposed administrators' efforts to feminize urban post offices in the 1890s and they continued, after 1900, to oppose efforts toward establishing equality of rank within the work force. Throughout the nineteenth century when administrators offered a rationale for their employment of women, they did so by expressing paternalistic solicitude for the "poor widow" or "dowryless single woman." They never expressed any belief in women's equal rights—based on abilities alone—to have access to jobs. That women were paid less than men even for the same work and were denied promotions to real positions of advancement was hardly inconsistent with these attitudes. Women filled a wider range of jobs by 1914 than they had in 1877, but they were as far as ever from being integrated into the work force as employees interchangeable with men.

On the other hand, from the view of the women who filled jobs in the P.T.T., it is clear that few women directly experienced the long-term changes in the character of postal employment. Rather, women from petit-bourgeois and working-class backgrounds perceived themselves better off in P.T.T. employment than they would have been in most traditional female jobs. Few women had initially sought independence through employment, and many *postières,* including and especially the many women who never married, may have regretted the circumstances that denied them a life devoted more exclusively to domestic tasks and responsibilities. Most women subscribed to the belief that woman's place, ideally, was in the home, and their inferior position in the work force reinforced that belief. Nonetheless, economic self-sufficiency was within reach of the experienced employee, and many women achieved, in addition, a small but not insignificant degree of upward mobility. Within both the A.G. and the separate *Association des Dames Employées,* women gained organizing experience and a greater sense of their strength as members of collective groups and as women. It seems likely that the economic contribution married women made to their households lessened their dependence on their husbands, and that some enjoyed the kind of companionate relationships experienced by *postier* couples like the Pechs and others.[1]

Generally, as telegraph or post office clerk or as participant in collective protests, women showed that they could perform a "man's job." They thereby placed a wedge, opening a breech however slim, in a social and moral order based on a sharp differentiation between the sexes. Despite the particularly obdurate character of old world societies, the *postières* had more choices than their mothers. Their lives in turn provided new measures against which their daughters and nieces judged their own experiences.

It took a disastrous war that drained France of its young men to break down certain restrictions on women's work and some die-hard attitudes about woman's place. By 1917, over 10,000 P.T.T. clerks had been mobilized, and there were no entrance examinations for men throughout the war. Overnight, hundreds of clerical positions were transformed into jobs for *dames employées,* including those of mail sorter and counter clerks in main post offices in Paris and the major provincial cities. Female *aides* brought in from secondary post offices in the countryside provided a ready supply of trained labor to fill vacated postal and telegraph jobs, and after the war they were named full-fledged *dames employées. Receveuses,* in the meantime, carried on their work as before, but often without the help of assistants, while a few women in the border regions performed heroic war deeds beyond the call of duty.[2]

Despite changes, however, the war failed to result immediately in an upgrading of women's status within the administration. Men rapidly promoted up through the ranks in the crisis continued to fill supervisory and even chief clerk positions. In the 1920s, militant women leaders, some from the old A.G., lost patience with their male colleagues and led an autonomous campaign aimed at obtaining equal pay for equal work. The result partly of these efforts, in 1928 women who had entered the administration before the war as *dames employées* were integrated into the ranks of "clerks," just as their male analogues, the "auxiliary clerks," had been three decades earlier. By the time the *dame employée* grade was assimilated with the male clerk grade, however, fewer and fewer women were being recruited as *dames employées* or men as clerks. Men and women alike were entering the administration in new, specialized "manipulative" grades, as mail sorters and telephone operators, with lower status, remuneration, and mobility than that enjoyed by men and women appointed to the same jobs before the war.[3]

Further, the end of the overtly discriminatory female grade did not eliminate sexual inequality in the administration. Today one of five employed Frenchwomen are civil servants, and over 142,000 women work for the Ministry of Postal Services and Telecommunications.[4] The diversity in the backgrounds, status, and situation of female employees is much greater than in the nineteenth and early twentieth centuries. A minority of women from middle-class backgrounds have in administrative positions, real professional opportunities unknown to earlier generations of women in the P.T.T. At the other extreme, however, and much greater in number are the women segregated in all female fields, like telephone and postal check services. These employees perform in large impersonal settings the most boring, repetitive and easily learned tasks which provide little training for a higher grade. Equally large numbers of women are employed in routine but more varied clerical jobs in post offices and administrative offices, where today women predominate. Regardless of their position, however, women in the P.T.T., like their female colleagues in other public services, earn less as a group than men with equivalent educations, and women also fill a disproportionately low number of the better-paying positions. The precise contours of women's work have changed along with the number of women employed by the postal services, but equality of opportunity and treatment remains elusive. Women occupy a larger space in the P.T.T. family, but they remain the poor sisters.

Abbreviations

ADC	Archives Départementales du Calvados
ADG	Archives Départementales de la Gironde
ADH	Archives Départementales du Hérault
ADN	Archives Départementales du Nord
AN	Archives Nationales
BMD	Bibliothèque Marguerite Durand
BN	Bibliothèque Nationale
BPT	Bibliothèque du Ministère des Postes et Télécommunications
BPTPV	Bibliothèque du Ministère des Postes et Télécommunicatons, Procès-verbaux du Conseil d'Administration de la Poste
CDRCB	Chambre des Députés, Rapport de la Commission du Budget
PP	Préfecture de Police (Paris)

Notes

Introduction

1. The best general survey of the history of women's work in England and France is Louise A. Tilly and Joan W. Scott, *Women, Work and Family* (New York, 1978). For the United States, see Alice Kessler-Harris, *Women Have Always Worked: A Historical Overview* (Old Westbury, N.Y., 1981).
2. An inspirational article for those of us interested in the feminization of clerical work was Margery Davies' "Woman's Place is at the Typewriter: the Feminization of the Clerical Labor Force," *Radical America* 8, no. 4 (July-August 1974):1–28. Also important was the general study of Lee Holcombe, *Victorian Ladies at Work: Middle-Class Working Women in England and Wales, 1850–1914* (Hamden, Conn., 1973). For a fine, recent description of the first female government workers in Washington, D.C., see Cindy S. Aron, " 'To Barter Their Souls for Gold': Female Clerks in Federal Government Offices, 1862–1890," *The Journal of American History* 67, (March 1981):835–53.
3. See, for example, Georges Dupeux, *La Soçiêtê Française, 1789–1970* (Paris, 1972), p. 159.
4. Throughout this study the term "post office manager" or the French title for the same has been used instead of "postmistress" or "postmaster" in order to avoid confusion. In France the *maître de poste* (fem. *maîtresse de poste*) owned and housed the horses and carriages needed for transporting the mail. The position was distinct from that of post office manager, though occasionally the same person filled both roles. The introduction of the railroad signaled the demise of the once very prosperous and socially powerful *maîtres de poste*. As shown in the interesting study of Madeleine Fouché, *La Poste aux chevaux de Paris et les maîtres à travers les siècles* (Paris, 1975), a woman—Louise Petit, widow of Jean-Nicholas Poulin—was *maîtresse de poste* for Paris between 1758 and 1776.

   While women have always managed small post offices in the United States, it is only very recently—in the 1960s—that they entered the clerical work force in significant numbers. The exclusion of women in U.S. cities reflects a combination of factors that distinguish U.S. postal services from European ones: these include the late introduction of merit exams in the United States, and the decentralization of recruitment policies permitting local postmasters, who were political appointees, a much greater say in the hiring of their clerical staffs. There was also the absence of a long tradition of the urbane, educated civil servant and incentives such as job security, regular pay raises, and retirement benefits which promoted, in Europe, more elitist standards of recruitment stressing general educational background rather than practical knowledge needed for postal work. The different demographics of the U.S. undoubtedly also played a role: though most U.S. clerks before World War II were native born, many were sons of immigrants.
5. Jeanne Bouvier, *Histoire des dames employées dans les postes, télégraphes et téléphones de 1714 à 1929* (Paris, 1930). When she wrote this book, Bouvier was a union militant advocating pay equality for women in the P.T.T.
6. For an excellent discussion of the legal determinants of women's position and how laws changed over the nineteenth century, see Esther S. Kanipe, "The Family, Private Pro-

perty and the State in France, 1870–1914'' (Ph.D. dissertation, University of Wisconsin-Madison, 1976).

7. Discussions of occupational segregation by sex particularly helpful to me include Valerie K. Oppenheimer, *The Female Labor Force in the United States* (Berkeley, 1970); selected articles in Martha Blaxall and Barbara Reagan, eds., *Women and the Workplace: The Implications of Occupational Segregation* (Chicago, 1976), with special mention to the article by Heidi Hartmann, ''Capitalism, Patriarchy, and Job Segregation by Sex,'' pp. 137–69; Ruth Milkman, ''Female Factory Labor and Industrial Structure: Control and Conflict over 'Woman's Place' in Auto and Electrical Manufacturing'' (Paper presented to the Women and Work seminar, Graduate Center-City University of New York, Fall 1982). Using different approaches and reaching conclusions with different emphases, all these writers attempt to determine what makes individual employers discriminate against women when it often appears in their best economic interests not to.

8. My findings on the different rates of women's employment in old and new jobs are supported by research on the British Post Office [see Samuel Cohn, ''Clerical Labor Intensity and the Feminization of Clerical Labor'' (Paper presented to the Women and Work seminar, Graduate Center-City University of New York, Fall 1982]. The distinction as to whether women were entering new jobs or jobs traditionally filled by men—regardless of the similarity in actual job tasks that may be involved—seems crucial to an understanding of the timing, dynamics, and implications of the feminization of clerical work.

Chapter One

1. Sophie Ulliac-Trémadeure, *Souvenirs d'une vieille Femme,* vol. 1 (Paris, 1861), pp. 160–64.
2. AN F⁹⁰ 20366, ''Liste des bureaux de poste de l'ancien régime et modifications intervenues dans leur fonctionnement, 1743–1793.''
3. Jeanne Bouvier, *Histoire des dames employées dans les P.T.T. de 1714 à 1929* (Paris, 1930), p. 17. For the history of postal services see Eugène Vaillé, *Histoire des Postes Françaises jusqu'à la Révolution* (Paris, 1946). While governed by the monarchy, postal services in the eighteenth century were exploited by *fermiers*—tax-collectors—who turned over to the state a percentage of the taxes levied on individuals for the conveyance of their letters, money and precious metals.
4. AN F⁹⁰ 20366, ''Liste des bureaux.'' Salaries for managers outside Paris ranged in the late 1780s from 4000 Livres for Lyon to 50 Livres for the smallest post offices.
5. Records (quoted in Bouvier, *Histoire des dames employées,* pp. 40–41, 185) show female mail carriers in the cities of Dunkerque and Valenciennes in the late eighteenth century. Usually succeeding deceased fathers or husbands, women continued into the nineteenth and early twentieth centuries to represent a small fraction of mail carriers in rural areas. Today female carriers are a familiar sight even in Paris.
6. AN F⁹⁰ 20366, ''Liste des bureaux.'' Half of all women's names on the list had the official title of *Veuve* (Widow) and four of five had either *Veuve* or *Madame,* which could signify either widowed or married.
7. Quoted in Octave Chevalier, ''Une famille de postiers bisontins, 1760–1848,'' *Revue des PTT* 19 (novembre-décembre 1964):30.
8. Ibid., pp. 28–31. Compare M. Pellégrino, ''Pendant plus d'un siècle une seule famille a géré le bureau de Bourg d'Oisans,'' *Revue des PTT* 15 (mai-juin), 1960:39–44.
9. AN F⁹⁰ 20221, ''Nomenclature des employés des Postes de Paris,'' 1735–1822.
10. Quoted in Bouvier, *Histoire des dames employées,* pp. 35–36.
11. AN F⁹⁰ 20368.
12. AN F⁹⁰ 20385, ''Recueils factices d'arrêtés en ampliations concernant des nominations de personnel dans l'ensemble du pays,'' 1814. In this year twenty of twenty-five women appointed obtained their positions through family ties whereas only seventeen of forty-two men followed this pattern.

13. After the state assumed control of the *Petite Poste* in 1780, the Postal Administration vacillated on the question of women's right to succeed male relatives in the city's services. Finally, the administration ruled in 1799 that positions in the *Petite Poste* "cannot be filled by women," and this decision remained in force (see Bouvier, *Histoire des dames employées*, pp. 21–22, 34).

14. AN F ^{90} 20367, "Nomenclature Générale des Bureaux de la Poste aux Lettres," 1806, 1820; "Nomenclature Générale des Bureaux de Poste," *Annuaire des Postes, 1834*.

15. *Annuaire des Postes, 1850*, p. 225.

16. Alexis Belloc, *Les Postes Françaises* (Paris, 1886), p. 452; *Instruction générale sur le service des Postes* (Paris, 1832–1833); Bouvier, *Histoire des dames employées*, p. 194.

17. *La France Administrative* 1 (1841): 316; AN F ^{90} 20367, "Nomenclature Générale des Bureaux," 1820; ADN P91/1, "Etat du personnel," 1841.

This view was furthered in Napoléon III's decree of 25 March 1852, which included *directrice de poste* on the list of public jobs filled through prefectual appointment. Though women were still in the minority in the Midi in 1841, they had clearly made inroads. In 1817, women were practically unheard of as *directrices* in this region: in that year none of the twelve post office managers in the Bouches du Rhônes was a woman, only one of twenty in the Gard, and one of eighteen in the Haute Garonne. By 1841 the number of *bureaux à taxation* run by women were respectively, five of twelve, nine of twenty, six of twenty-three. In comparison, certain departments of northern France already had a significant proportion of female managers by 1817: women ran twenty-one of forty post offices in the Seine-et-Oise, seven of twenty-five in Seine Inférieure, and nine of twenty-seven in the Nord. In 1841 the number of *bureaux à taxation* run by women in these departments were respectively, fifty of fifty-two, thirty of thirty-six, twenty-two of thirty-three.

19. *Bulletin des Lois*, XXIX, no. 1162, "Ordonnance du Roi portant sur l'Organisation de l'Administration Centrale du Ministre des Finances," pp. 1177–78; *Instruction générale sur le service des Postes* (Paris, 1856), Article 40.

20. *Bulletin des Lois*, XXIX, no. 1162, "Ordonnance du Roi," pp. 1177–78.

21. *Instruction générale, 1856*, Article 40.

22. *La France Administrative* 2 (1842): 381; *Annuaire des Postes, 1860; Annuaire des Postes, 1880*.

23. Julie Daubié, *La Femme Pauvre au XIXe Siècle* (Paris, 1866), p. 197.

24. *La France Administrative* 1 (1841):213; 3 (1843):247–48.

25. Ibid. 1 (1841):215; 4 (1844):545–46.

26. Ibid. 1 (1841):287; 316–17; 2 (1842):338–41.

27. Ibid. 1 (1840):57; 2 (1841):85–86; 3 (1843):193.

28. *La Gazette des Femmes*, 7 août 1841. Compare to the feminist arguments posed by one *directrice* in a letter to *France Administrative* [1 (1841):250–51], the only contribution to the journal from a woman.

29. *Bulletin mensuel des Postes* 89, (septembre 1863) ("Circulaire no. 317, Bureau de personnel"), p. 383.

30. *Annuaire des Postes, 1880*. Based on a 10 percent sample of bureau/title-holder listings.

31. Edouard Charton, *Dictionnaire des Professions*, 3rd ed. (Paris, 1880), p. 430; Maurice Block, *Dictionnaire de l'administration française*, 2nd ed. (Paris, 1878), p. 966.

32. *La Revue des Postes* 17 (7 juin 1893):79–80; ADN P91/10, Letter, janvier 1880.

Chapter Two

1. *Le Journal des Postes et des Télégraphes* 7 (1884), quoted in Bouvier, *Histoire des dames employées*, p. 197.

2. ADN P91/1, Letters, 18 février 1870, 12 février 1870.

3. ADN P91/1, Letters, 8 novembre 1867, 30 avril 1870; ADN P91/13, Letter, 20 août 1866; ADN P91/12, Letter, 4 septembre 1884.

4. ADN P91/12, Petition, 15 janvier 1885.

5. Edith Thomas, *Pauline Roland* (Paris, 1956), pp. 33–35, 45–48.

6. *La France Administrative* 1 (1841):316 and appointment lists, 1843–1844; AN F^{90} 20511-20530 and unclassified, employee records of functionaries born before 1865, and 1865 to 1870. Unless otherwise noted, statistics below on employees' backgrounds and employment patterns have been derived from data obtained from these work records.

7. *La Gazette Nationale*, 29 novembre 1789.

8. M. Telrouc, *Boutades postales* (Paris, 1873), p. 14; *Le Journal des Postes et des Télégraphes 4* (1 novembre 1868):9–13; Léon Brasier, *Histoire des Maisons d'Education de la Légion d'Honneur* (Paris, 1912).

9. ADN P91/10, Letter, 10 juin 1882.

10. Henri Issanchou, *Le livre d'or des Postes* (Paris, 1885), pp. 215ff.

11. ADN P91/14, "Renseignements," c. 1880. This report lists the following husbands' occupations: coal mine manager, factory sales representative, retired army captain, notary's clerk, health officer, unemployed. Manuscript censuses for the Seine in the 1890s show the following breakdown occupations of husbands of *receveuses* who, for the most part, began employment in the 1870s and 1880s: six postal employees, three railroad clerks, two schoolteachers, two other civil servants, one writer, one retired colonel, one draftsman, five unemployed (retired or property-owners).

12. *Annuaire des Postes, 1850, Annuaire des Postes, 1880*. Pèrcentages based on 20 percent and 10 percent samples of bureau/title-holder listings for 1850 and 1880, respectively.

13. ADH P, unclassified, "Renseignements," 1889; manuscript censuses for the Seine, 1891, 1896. The sources show the low fertility rate of *receveuses,* whose tendency to have few children was related to late marriages and reflected the general trend for civil servants. Forty percent of married or widowed *receveuses* aged thirty to forty-four in these two departments had no children, 30 percent had one child, 23 percent had two children, and only 7 percent more than two children. The figures for all married and widowed *receveuses* (totalling sixty-four) regardless of age were, respectively, 36 percent, 27 percent, 22 percent, and 16 percent.

14. Existing employee records for 1,666 *receveuses* show that 92 percent remained in the work force for more than twenty years. While this particular set of records does not include all employees, and is probably biased toward *receveuses* with longer records, other evidence, such as personnel lists, suggest that the bias was not very deep.

15. ADN P91/10, Letter, 10 juin 1882.

16. The test was roughly as difficult as the examination for the *certificat d'études primaires* awarded in public schools for the completion of primary studies. Handwriting, spelling, writing skills, geography, and arithmetic were tested. The test was given periodically in the department *prefectures* before a committee of three persons, two postal supervisors and for reasons of propriety, one woman, usually a schoolteacher or directress. [See A. Barnier, *Manuel des postulants aux recettes de début* (Digne, 1883); pp. 12–62; ADN P91/5, Commission d'examen, 1852; ADH P, unclassified, "Examen pour la candidature aux bureaus de poste aux lettres," 1880.]

17. J. G. Borrel, *Les recettes simples: Conseils aux candidats, aux aides, et aux receveuses* (Paris, 1886), p. 97.

18. Louis Frank, *La femme dans les emplois publics* (Brussels, 1893), p. 11.

19. "Relêvê des mesures disciplinaires," *Bulletin mensuel des Postes,* (septembre 1855):17; 99 (novembre 1863):614–15. Employee records show instances of *receveuses* either suspended from functions or "permanently" removed from employment, then reinstated.

20. S. de Lange, *Au Service du Public durant quarante ans 1887–1926* (Lyon, 1929), pp. 250–52.

21. Ernest Legouvé, *La Femme en France au XIXe Siècle* (Paris, 1873), pp. 129–30.

22. *La France Administrative* 2 (1842):338–41.

23. BPT, *La Mosaïque,* pp. 210–12.

24. ADN P91/14, "Renseignements," c. 1880.

25. ADN P91/1, Letter of Marie Delannoy, 16 octobre 1885.

26. ADN P91/12, Letter of Mme Vve Delgrang, 8 mai 1884.
27. ADN P91/14, "Renseignements," c. 1880; ADN P91/14, Letter, 25 janvier 1880, entitled "mes appréciations intimes sur les receveuses des postes" from a *sous-préfect* who first refused on principle to give information regarding the *receveuses'* politics and then, on second thought, viewed as absurd the very idea that as women they might have political beliefs.
28. For example, the case of Mme Héon, *receveuse* at Dozulé (Calvados) whose mayor accused her of "negligence and reproached her . . . for never having given him an official letter . . . and for generally transmitting his correspondance only after inexplicable delays." Depite the *receveuse's* expression of repentance, the mayor requested an investigation. Six months later, the departmental director ruled in the *receveuse's* favor. "Mme Héon is noted for having a cantankerous disposition," he observed. "But I find nothing unfavorable in her file with regard to her probity and honorability." Since the *receveuse* Héon was sixty-one years old and was to retire the next year, the director decided to maintain her in the same residence (ADC M247, *Pièces* 237–46, février-juillet 1897). But sometimes conflicts went too far for such resolutions. In another instance, the *receveuse*, a widow with eighteen years' service, was accused of insulting the local tax collector who in turn accused her of negligence of duty. Despite the "exaggeration in the complaint" against the *receveuse*, the director recommended her transfer, because her position in the community was no longer tenable. The whole affair had "embittered her character," and she had been the object of denunciations accusing her of opening letters, reading postcards, and having intimate relations with one of the mail carriers (ADN P91/12, Letter, 19 novembre 1886). For examples of cases involving politics, see ADN P91/12, Letter, 2 mars 1885; ADN P91/10, Letter, juillet 1881; ADN P91/9, Letter, 22 fevrier 1878; ADC M247, *Pièces* 320–327, juin–juillet 1880.
29. *Le Journal des Postes* 8 (1 décembre 1872), cited in Bouvier, *Histoire des dames employées*, pp. 99–100.
30. *Journal des Postes* 6 (1 janvier 1869):10–11.
31. Lange, *Au Service du Public*, pp. 250–52.
32. For cases of the former, see *Bulletin mensuel des Postes* 80 (avril 1862): 186; 111 (novembre 1864): 605; 116 (avril 1865): 197. For examples of the latter, see 3 (novembre 1855): 116; *La Revue des Postes* 8 (1 juin 1884):84–85; ADC M247, *Pièces* 330–31, janvier 1890.
33. *Le Journal des Postes et des Télégraphes* 16 (6 août 1893).
34. "Relêvé des mesures disciplinaires," *Bulletin mensuel des Postes*, 1855–1865; and Borrel, *Les recettes simples*, p. 111.
35. *Le Journal des Postes*, 1866–1875.
36. Employee record of Jeanne Marie Longaygues, born 5 October 1844.
37. *Annuaire des Postes, 1890;* Millerand, CDRCB, Exercise 1892, Impression No. 1633 (Paris, 1891), pp. 95–96.
38. Employee record of Marie Eugénie Lissot, born 20 June 1858.
39. See, for example, ADN P91/13, Poillot File, Letters, 2 décembre 1867 to 7 août 1873.
40. *Le Journal des Postes et des Télégraphes* 10 (13 août 1887).
41. Ibid. 10 (27 août 1887).
42. See below, p. 57.

Chapter Three

1. Eugène Vaillé, *Histoire des Postes Françaises*, vol. 2 (Paris, 1947); Boudenoot, CDRCB, Exercise 1896, Impression No. 2701 (Paris, 1897), p. 87. The best report on the causes and effects of the merger is Adolphe Cochery, *Rapport présenté à M. le Président de la République* (Paris, 1884).

2. Cochery, *Rapport*, pp. 53, 57–58.
3. Albert Cim, *Bureaux et Bureaucrates, mémoires d'un employé des P.T.T.* (Paris, 1910), pp. 41, 116.
4. For the biographies of writer-employees see Issanchou, *Le Livre d'Or des Postes.*
5. Ed. Vandal, *Rapport au Ministre des Finances sur le service des Postes, janvier, 1866* (Paris, 1866), pp. 41–42.
6. Conflicting statistics make it difficult to determine the precise number of clerks. Millerand (CDRCB, pp. 95–96) reported in 1891 the following numbers of clerks in "outside" offices: 1,554 chief clerks, 7,742 clerks, and 2,740 "auxiliary clerks" (whose introduction is discussed below).
7. Cochery, *Rapport*, pp. 52, 143, 158.
8. *Annuaire des Postes, 1877, Annuaire des Postes, 1890.* In 1883 there were 1,262 ambulatory clerks, most of whom worked out of Paris. For descriptions of the duties and work of different kinds of clerks, see below and Paul Jaccottey, *Traité de Législation et d'exploitation postales* (Paris, 1891); Benjamin Laurent, *Services postaux en 1913. L'organisation administrative, le sydicalisme postale* (Saint-Etienne, 1913).
9. Cochery, *Rapport*, p. 51.
10. For examples of examinations, see J. G. Borrel, *Guide pratique des candidats aux emplois de surnuméraires, commis auxiliaires, de dames télégraphistes et téléphonistes* (Paris, 1884). In practice, political patronage was still sometimes a factor in appointments, though such interference was much less common than was true for positions filled though prefects' appointments, that of *receveuse* or pre-merger telegraph clerk, for example.
11. *La Revue des Postes* 12 (1 août 1888):114–15; ADH P, unclassified, "Notices sur les candidats surnuméraires," 1892–1895. In the 1891 *concours* there were fifty-two *bacheliers* who represented only 2.8 percent of all candidates that year, see *Le Journal des Postes et des Télégraphes* 15 (6 decembre 1892).
12. As noted retrospectively in *Le Courrier des Examens* 15 (30 octobre 1903):698. The same proposal failed again in 1903.
13. Cochery, *Rapport*, p. 43.
14. An analysis of 4,880 employee records for men born before 1859 (most of whom entered employment before the merger) shows that 32.4 percent of all clerks nationally came from the twenty-nine departments south of a line cutting across France at La Rochelle and St. Etienne and west of Nîmes (this region hereafter defined as the "southwest"). The figure for 9,885 men born 1859 to 1870 was 34.8 percent. In both periods men from the southwest were over-represented in the work force; this region comprised only 27 percent of the total French population according to the 1866 census. Only 5 to 6 percent of all clerks in each cohort were born in Paris, the department of the Seine, or the Seine-et-Oise combined.
15. Employee records provided birthdates and birthplaces; birth records were used to obtain parents' occupations. Because birth records are decentralized in the departments, it was necessary to select Paris and the three departments of the Nord, Gironde, and Hérault. These were chosen because of their variations in industrial development and urbanization, the existence of a high enough number of employees to give a good return, and other practical considerations. Although men from Paris were not typical of the work force, which relied heavily on men from provincial small towns, a breakdown of the social origins of the Parisians nevertheless serves as a particularly good bellweather for evaluating long term recruitment trends such as the proletarianization of the work force. The table below shows the father's occupation (or if unknown, mother's occupation) of clerks born in Paris and the three departments. Most men born before 1859 entered postal and telegraph services before the 1878 merger.

Father's Occupation of Male Clerks (percentages)

Birthplace

Occupational Category	Paris		Nord		Hérault		Gironde	
(percentages)	(1)*	(2)**	(1)	(2)	(1)	(2)	(1)	(2)
Professional	7.4	7.0	–	2.4	3.0	2.1	8.3	–
Shopkeeping	17.6	10.4	10.6	15.8	10.6	22.1	16.7	20.0
Public Sector	30.6	23.5	31.9	29.3	19.7	11.6	8.3	25.7
Employee	18.5	23.5	8.5	11.0	6.1	6.3	11.1	2.9
Artisanal	21.3	19.1	23.4	24.4	36.4	26.3	30.6	31.4
Unskilled worker	–	4.3	10.6	3.7	1.5	4.2	2.8	2.9
Domestic, other service	1.9	7.0	2.1	1.2	–	3.2	2.8	2.9
Agriculture	–	–	12.8	12.2	21.2	21.1	19.4	14.3
Other, no profession	2.8	5.2	–	–	1.5	3.2	–	–
Total	100%	100%	100%	100%	100%	100%	100%	100%
Number	(108)	(115)	(47)	(82)	(66)	(95)	(36)	(35)

* (1) Men born before 1859
** (2) Men born before 1859-1864

16. For example, 49 percent of clerks born in the Nord between 1859 and 1870 had their careers interrupted by military services, and the figures were respectively, 43 percent, 33 percent, and 55 percent for men born in the Hérault, Gironde, and Paris. That some clerks did three to five years of military service, other just one year or none at all, reflects the unfairness of recruitment laws (which enabled men of means to avoid the ar-.my or serve for a shorter period), and it also points up disparities in backgrounds and wealth of clerks which affected men's careers. Particularly long absences were detrimental to a clerk's career and, regardless of the duration of duty, many experienced delays in being reintegrated into the work force. As a group, clerks were more mobile than *receveuses* (see above, Chapter Two): more than half of all clerks changed residences more than three times, and almost one-fifth moved eight or more times.
17. Cochery, *Rapport,* pp. 52, 158.
18. Ibid. By 1890 women worked in telegraph centrals in fifteen cities, the new locales including Angers, Bourg, La Rochelle, Le Havre, Rennes, Rodez, St. Etienne, Alger, see *Le Courrier des Examens* 2 (1890):443.
19. "Une enquête sur le service télégraphique en Angleterre," *Annales Télégraphiques* 3 (janvier-février, 1876):5-8; "La Réduction du Tarif Télégraphique et los moyens de la réaliser," *La Revue Scientifique de la France et de l'Etranger 6 (9 decembre 1876):571; BPT TD60, Report from the Select Committee on Post Office (Telegraph Department),* translated in 1881; BPT TD237, "Angleterre, Télégraphes, mss. traduit à la Direction du cabinet et du service central, 'Le bureau télégraphique de Londres,' tiré du journal *Verkehrszeitung,* 7 July 1882."

20. *Report by Mr. Scudamore on the Reorganization of the Telegraph System of the United Kingdom* (London, 1871); Cochery, *Rapport*, p. 53.
21. Employee records; *La Revue de Postes* 6 (1 avril 1882):50–51.
22. Of the 1,365 women born between 1859 and 1870 and who began their employment in Paris, 46 percent were born in Paris or the suburbs constituting the department of the Seine. With the wider use of provincial women in the 1890s (see below), the percentage dropped to 38 percent (for 992 women born 1871–1875). Throughout the period the proportion of Parisians in the Paris work force remained much higher than was true for men.
23. *La Revue des Postes* 16 (21 septembre 1892):299–308.
24. Ludger Collet, *Des conditions du Travail dans l'Administration des Postes et des Télégraphes* (Paris, 1910), p. 90.
25. Léon Riant, *Rapport sur l'Administration des Postes présenté au Ministre des Finances* (Paris, 1877), p. 90.
26. Cochery, *Rapport*, pp. 52, 158; *La Revue des Postes* 12 (12 décembre 1888):193-94; BPT TG2, "Notes prises au cours de M. Froüin," p. 135.
27. "The employment of women in the postal service," *L'Union Postale Internationale* (Berne, 1876), pp. 254, 260–70. Some women were also employed as urban clerks in the United States; the city of Boston was specifically mentioned in the report. It seems that by the end of the century, women post office clerks were exceptional in American cities, according to Marshall Cushing, *The Story of our Post Office* (Boston, 1893), p. 180.
28. *La Revue des Postes* 11 (16 novembre 1887):171. There were also translated reports of the experience with women clerks in Britain; see, for example, BPT PD564, "Documents relatifs au service des Postes et des Télégraphes," pp. 253-59, 265-74.
29. *La Revue des Postes* 6 (2 juin 1882):84; *Le Journal des Postes 3 (31 janvier 1880)*. Compare *Le Revue des Postes* 13 (11 décembre 1889):393-94 in which one writer reasserted women's superior skills.
30. *La Revue des Postes* 12 (1 septembre 1888):130.
31. Alexis Belloc, *La Télégraphie historique depuis les temps les plus reculées jusqu'à nos jours* (Paris, 1888).
32. The engraving of one of the first French telephone bureaus, in *La Science populaire* (1880, p. 325) shows only men at work, suggesting that in the very beginning of the services, France may have used men operators. See also, Brenda Maddox, "Women and the Switchboard," in *The Social Impact of the Telephone,* ed. Ithiel de Sola Pool (Cambridge, Mass., 1977), pp. 262–80; and Brenda Maddox, "A woman's place is at the switchboard," *New Scientist,* 18 March 1976, pp. 614–15 in BMD DOS/350/FON. The telephone was invented in 1876. In the United States and Britain, boys were used in the first commercial exchanges established in 1878 but were found unsatisfactory. Maddox writes: "The boys it seemed were rude. They talked back to subscribers, played tricks with the wires, took St. Patrick's Day off, and in the words of one of the early female operators, were 'complete and consistent failures.' "
    France briefly experimented with the use of boys as young telegraph messengers in one telephone bureau in 1900, but the boys, for reasons that are difficult to document, did not work out. The effort itself is understandable in the context of the opposition to the feminization of jobs around 1900 and the high rate of illness among women employees (see below) as well as the desire to cut labor costs.
33. There are few traces in the employee journals of a negative reaction to women's employment in these offices, though some men employees must have resented the intrusion. The hero of the semi-autobiographical novel, *Les Cartons verts* (Paris, 1901) by George Lecomte, a clerk in central administration, describes the female employees disdainfully: "for the most part without graces or beauty . . . most often pretentious, very *brevet supérieur* or shrewish. They dress with negligence and wear cheap perfume. Their fingers are stained with ink and become quickly dried with yellow wrinkles from shuffling papers."

34. Cochery, *Rapport,* pp. 57–58; Ministère du Commerce, Direction Générale des Postes. Documents Statistiques (Paris, 1894), pp. 14–17; *La Revue des Postes* 16 (21 septembre 1892):308.
35. Figures for 1880 based on Charton, *Dictionnaire des Professions,* p. 430; for 1892, my estimate is based on number of post offices and later figures for *aides.*
36. ADH P, unclassified, Confidential Circular from Cochery to all departmental prefects, 22 février 1882. To justify seizing control of appointments, the Postal Administration argued that the 1852 decree applied only to post offices proper, not to merged postal/telegraph bureaus.
37. Employee records show the following breakdown for women with family titles listed: 38 percent the relatives of postal employees; 15 percent of schoolteachers, 27 percent of military or police; 12 percent of tax collectors or other fiscal officers; 4 percent of mayors or adjoints; 3 percent, other.
38. ADC M250, Personnel, Postes et Télégraphes, "Notices," 1890–1894.
39. ADN P91/10, Letter, janvier 1880.
40. *La Revue des Postes* 9 (1 mars 1885):33–34.
41. ADC M250 (deuxième partie), "Candidats receveurs," 15 juillet 1892; ADH P, unclassified, "Tableau de classement des candidats receveurs," 15 novembre 1890.
42. *Le Journal des Postes et des Télégraphes* 16 (5 février 1893). A help wanted ad for *aide* offered a salary of 800 francs plus lodging for a bureau in a Paris suburb.
43. Statistics for postal circulation from Boudenoot, CDRCB, p. 87. Between 1887 and 1889 the Postal Administration was once again brought under the aegis of the Finance Ministry. To see the effects of budget cuts on postal services and personnel during this period, see Chamber of Deputy budget reports.
44. Mesureur, CDRCB, Exercise 1893, Impression No. 2323 (Paris, 1892), p. 151; BPTPV, 20 novembre 1888; *La Revue des Postes* 14 (20 août 1890):265.
45. *Le Journal des Postes* 14 (23 mars 1891). No *concours* at all was held during four years (1884, 1888–1890). In 1885, 4,158 men took the examination to fill only 347 places. The number of candidates was respectively 3,695 and 2,817 for 1886 and 1887 for equally few or fewer places.
46. Thus, comparing the cohort of men born 1859–1864 to those born 1865–1870, one sees that the proportion of men born in Paris whose fathers were artisans increased from 19.1 percent (of 115 total) to 30.5 percent (of 177 total) and sons of unskilled workers from 4.3 percent to 7.3 percent. For the Nord, the figures were 24.4 percent (of 82 total) to 32.8 percent (of 119 total) for artisans' sons, and 3.7 to 5.9 percent for unskilled workers' sons; for the Hérault, 26.3 percent (of 95 total) to 40.7 percent (of 52 total) for artisans' sons, and 4.2 percent to 7.7 percent for unskilled workers' sons; and for the Gironde, 31.4 percent (of 35 total) to 40.9 percent (of 44 total) for artisans' sons, and 2.9 percent to 4.5 percent for unskilled workers' sons. The percentage of men from agricultural backgrounds either decreased or remained unchanged, reflecting the greater recruitment of auxiliaries in cities and the relative financial well-being of the peasants who normally sent sons into civil service employment.
47. See Susan D. Bachrach, "Parisian Postal Clerks and the Depression of the 1880s," Paper read at the twenty-eighth annual meeting of the Society for French Historical Studies, 26 March 1982.
48. *Journal officiel,* Chambre des députés, 21 novembre 1891, pp. 457–58; 7–8 février, 1893, pp. 567–600.
49. Noulens, CDRCB, Exercise 1908, Impression No. 1247 (Paris, 1907), p. 136.
50. *Journal officiel,* Chambre des députés, 21 novembre 1891, comments of M. Raiberti, pp. 455–56.
51. *Le Courrier des Examens* 1 (1 mai 1889:36; 6 (1 septembre 1894):257.
52. BPT TG2, "Notes," p. 121.
53. Millerand, CDRCB, p. 127. A total of 110 post offices opened nationally between 1887 and 1890, compared to an annual increase of 100 or more for 1879–1886.
54. Mesureur, CDRCB, pp. 39–40. As a result, in a northern department like Calvados, the

aides ranked on the appointment list in 1891 had spent on the average more than five years as *aide;* in the southern department of the Hérault, the length of time was the same and, worse, the top ten candidates on the list of 55 names for four appointments had worked on average over eight years as *aide* (see note 41).

55. *La Revue des Postes* 16 (6 janvier 1892):2; 15 (28 septembre 1891):306-07.
56. *Journal officiel,* Chambre des députés, 21 novembre 1891, p. 451.
57. Mesureur, CDRCB, p. 42; *La Revue des Postes* 17 (15 novembre 1893):364; *Bulletin mensuel des Postes et des Télégraphes* 15 (décembre 1892);1302.
58. Mesureur, CDRCB, p. 42.
59. *La Revue des Postes* is the source throughout this discussion for the chronology of the feminization policy. *Annuaire des Poste* listings of post offices provided addresses, bureau classifications, etc.
60. *La Revue des Postes* 16 (11 mai 1892):150.
61. *Le Journal des Postes et des Télégraphes* 15 (20 novembre 1892).

Chapter Four

1. See cartoon entitled "Demoiselles aus bureaux de poste," from *L'Illustration,* reprinted in Georges Brunel, *La Poste à Paris* (Amiens, 1920), p. 351; *Le Journal des Postes,* 5 novembre 1893.
2. *L'Eclair,* 30 octobre 1893; compare reaction of "Garonne journal" quoted in *Le Journal des Postes et des Télégraphes* 16 (4 mars 1894).
3. *Le Journal des Femmes,* avril 1894.
4. *Le Petit Journal,* 5 septembre 1894.
5. *La Paix,* 4 août 1894,·p. 2.
6. Charles Sowerwine, "Women and Socialism in France 1871-1921: Socialist Women's Groups from Léonie Rouzade to Louise Saumoneau" (Ph.D. dissertation, University of Wisconsin-Madison, 1973), pp. 99-100.
7. *Le Journal des Femmes* 2 (décembre 1892):1-3 (décembre 1893):1; *Le Temps,* 28 octobre 1891, p. 3.
8. Seè, for example, *La Revue des Postes* 16 (1 juin 1892):172; 16 (22 juin 1892):197; 16 (21 septembre 1892):308.
9. *Le Journal des Postes et des Télégraphes* 15 (23 juillet 1892).
10. Georges Stat, "Une idée géniale," *L'Union des Postes* 3 (juillet 1892):2.
11. "Les Joyeusetés de la Féminisation," *L'Union des Postes* 4 (novembre 1893):2-3; *La Revue des Postes* 17 (13 décembre 1893):395; H. Melven, "Conséquences," *L'Union des Postes* 6 (avril 1895):1-2; "Les Bienfaits de la Féminisation des Bureaux de Poste," *République de Seine et Marne,* 14 novembre 1895, reprinted in *La Revue des Postes* 19 (4 décembre 1895):389-90.
12. "Guichetier à Paris," "Les Bureaux Composés de Femmes," *Le Journal des Postes et des Télégraphes* 15 (28 mai 1892).
13. *La Revue des Postes* 17 (11 octobre 1893):323-24; BPT TA6, 1892, p. 21. A typical complaint regarding service in post offices was that of deputy Eugène Mir who declared in 1890 that "one has but to appear any day in a postal bureau in Paris to realize that it is necessary to wait a quarter of an hour, a half hour, sometimes longer before being served" *(Journal officiel,* Débats de la Chambre des députés, 17 novembre 1890, p. 476).
14. *La Revue des Postes* 11 (16 novembre 1887):171. This rumor accompanied rumors of the feminization, which never occurred at this earlier date.
15. *Le Journal des Postes et des Télégraphes* 15 (28 mai 1892).
16. Stat, "Une idée génial," p. 2.
17. *Le Journal des Postes et des Télégraphes* 17 (17 juin 1894).
18. Ibid. 15:711 (16 juillet 1892).
19. *La Revue des Postes* 26 (24 février 1897):57-58. Compare *Le Journal des Postes et des*

Télègraphes 16 (22 janvier 1893); C. Benise, "Du role de la Femme dans la sociêtê actuelle," Ibid. 16 (24 septembre 1893); Ibid. 16 (1 octobre 1893); *La Revue des Postes* 19 (27 fevrier 1895):70.

20. *Le Journal des Postes et des Télègraphes* 17 (17 juin 1894), 15 (16 juillet 1892).
21. Ibid. 16 (12 février 1893; 16 (19 février 1893).
22. The statistics in Table 1 reflect the different occupational structures and degrees of urbanization of the three departments and mirror the kinds of alternative employment opportunities for educated women in these departments. Thus the higher proportion of women born in the Hérault to professionals and civil servants is best explained as the result of the small number of postal jobs open for women in the department, the small number of alternative jobs for educated women, and the limited employment possibilities for men, who entered postal employment and other public administration jobs in disproportionate numbers. One might expect this same pattern for. other highly agricultural departments which sent relatively few women into postal employment during this period.
23. According to *Le Journal des Débats* (5 août 1894) in that year more than half of the candidates had their *brevet simple* and 15 percent of the total their *brevet supérieur*. In the departments of the Calvados and Hérault, about one-fourth of all candidates in the early 1890s were reported as having the *brevet simple* and 3 to 4 percent, the *brevet supérieur*. Since all diplomas were not systematically reported in the departmental sources, however, the latter figure is probably an underestimate (ADC M250, "Notices"; ADH P, unclassified, "Candidates Dames Employées.")
24. ADC M250, "Notices," 19 février 1903.
25. ADC M250, "Notices," 17 août 1898.
26. ADC M250, "Notices," 6 février 1891 and employee record of Mlle De Than born 28 December 1869 in Thaon (Calvados); ADG 6P162 ff., 1905.
27. ADC M250, "Notices"; ADH P, unclassified "Candidates Dames Employées."
28. Husbands' occupations derived from election lists and *Annuaires des Poste;* ADG 6P162-6P192, "Renseignements, mariage." For attitudes regarding the reluctance even of some postal and telegraph clerks to marry women without dowries from the administration, see "Le mariage d'un timide," *Petit Journal,* supplément illustré, 4 juillet 1897, p. 211.
29. See above, p. 26.
30. ADC M250, "Notice" for Albertine Létirand, 17 avril 1894, provides one example. One of the questions on the prefects' report concerned the ability of the candidate to provide for herself during the apprenticeship period.
31. *Le Journal des Postes et des Télègraphs* 17 (26 août 1894).
32. "Les Ronds-de-Cuir Féminins," *La Revue des Postes* 19 (27 février 1895):70. See Peter V. Meyers, "From Conflict to Cooperation: Men and Women Teachers in the Belle Epoque," *Historical Reflections* 7, no. 2–3 (1980):493–505.
33. "Les Recettes Simples de Début," *La Revue des Postes* 17 (7 juin 1891):179–80.
34. See Madeleine Guilbert, *Les femmes et l'organisation syndicale avant 1914* (Paris, 1966); and Madeleine Guilbert, *Fonctions des Femmes dans l'Industrie* (Paris, 1966).
35. *Journal officiel,* Débats de la Chambre des députés, 14 janvier 1898, p. 23; Vogeli, CDRCB, Exercise 1898 (Paris, 1897), p. 10.
36. "Déménagement Perpétuel," *L'Union des Postes,* 3 (décembre 1892); *La Revue des Postes* 18 (10 janvier 1894):10; Ibid. 17 (20 novembre 1893):369–70; *Le Journal des Postes et des Télègraphes* 16 (22 janvier 1893), 17 (25 février 1894); 17 (11 mars 1894). ADH P, unclassified, Letter dated 5 octobre 1900 from a clerk, "married and native of Pézenas" and employed in the post office of Pézenas; the clerk "had heard" that his bureau was going to be "feminized," asked the mayor of the town to determine if the rumor were true, and received the reassuring answer that the rumor was unfounded.
37. *La Revue des Postes* 17 (18 janvier 1893): 21; *Le Journal des Postes et des Télègraphes* 15 (6 décembre 1892); 17 (11 mars 1894).
38. *La Revue des Postes* 20 (19 février 1896):58–59.

39. Kératry, *Rapport présenté à la commission extra-parlementaire des postes et des télégraphes* (Paris, 1911), p. 491.
40. *L'Union des Postes* 3 (janvier 1892):3; 9(31 juillet 1898): 1.
41. *Compte definitif des dépenses de l'exercise* (Paris) for 1890 and 1898 show that the number of women in urban postal and telegraph services increased from 902 to 3,565. As a basis for comparison to the men, I have purposively excluded the 1,531 women employed in telephone work by 1898. On evidence of the same sources and an estimate of the number of auxiliary clerks employed in 1890, it appears that the number of ordinary and auxiliary clerks combined dropped by 13 to 15 percent (from about 9,641 to 8,197) while the number of chief clerks employed in postal, telegraph, and ambulatory services increased by 28 percent, from 1,276 to 1,636.

Chapter Five

1. Quoted in *La Revue des Postes* 17 (1 novembre 1893):345-46.
2. Quoted in *Le Journal des Postes et des Télégraphes* 17 (5 août 1894).
3. Letter signed "an old *receveur,*" *Le Journal des Postes et des Télégraphes* 19 (1 mars 1896).
4. Mesureur, CDRCB, Exercise 1894, Impression No. 2846 (Paris, 1893), pp. 16–17.
5. *La Paix,* 4 août· 1894. Compare *Le Gaulois,* cited in *Le Journal des Postes et des Télégraphes* 17 (6 mai 1894).
6. BPTPB, PA721, PB174, 17 avril 1888, 29 septembre 1888, 20 novembre 1888, 19 novembre 1889.
7. Mesureur, CDRCB, Exercise 1895, Impression No. 966 (Paris, 1894), p. 43; *Journal officiel,* Débats de la Chambre des députés, 7 février 1893, comment of deputy Gillot, pp. 574–75; Vogeli, CDRCB, Exercise 1897, Impression No. 2044 (Paris, 1896), pp. 123–24.
8. *Le Journal des Postes et des Télégraphes* 17 (28 janvier 1894).
9. Mesureur, CDRCB, Exercise 1894, p. 16.
10. Mesureur, CDRCB, Exercise 1895, pp. 40–43, annexe no. 7.
11. Vogeli, CDRCB, Exercise 1897, pp. 17–24.
12. See below, p. 83.
13. Quoted in *La Revue des Postes* 21 (3 fevrier 1897):35.
14. BPTPV, 3 novembre 1887, 22 novembre 1887, 29 novembre 1887, 7 février 1888.
15. *Journal officiel,* Débats de la Chambe des députés, 7 février 1895, pp. 257-58.
16. Ibid., 2 décembre 1896, p. 743.
17. Edith Taïeb, *Hubertine Auclert, La Citoyenne, 1848–1914 (Paris, 1982).*
18. From *Libre Parole,* reprinted in *Le Journal des Postes et des Télégraphes* 17 (26 août 1894).
19. *Le Journal des Femmes* 3 (avril 1894); 3 (30 mai 1894); 6 (novembre 1897); 9 (mai 1900). In its 1893 list of demands presented to the Chamber of Deputies, *La Ligue* placed second on the list "equal salary for state employees of both sexes" (Ibid., novembre 1893).
20. Bouvier, *Histoire des dames employées* pp. 142–74, and later works derived from Bouvier, such as Marie-Hélène Zylberberg-Hocquard, *Féminisme et Syndicalisme en France* (Paris, 1978), p. 54.
21. Quoted in Vogeli, Exercise 1897, p. 22. Compare *La Revue des Postes* 21 (3 février 1897):35.
22. *L'Union des Postes* 6 (avril 1895): 1–2. For negative assessments of the policy by individual *receveurs,* see *L'Union des Postes* 7 (30 septembre 1897): 1–2; 12 (31 août 1901):3–4. For opinions of departmental directors, see BPT PB173, "Question des Aides."
23. Based on personnel/bureau listings in *Annuaire des Postes, 1900.*
24. "La Féminisation Postale," *La petite République,* 2 mars 1894, p. 1: "Les résultats

qu'attendait l'Administration supérieur des Postes en remplaçant le personnel masculin par des employées-dames sont, paraît-il, tout autres que ceux qu'on espérait.

Les plaintes du public causées par l'insuffisance professionnelle des gentes demoiselles préposées aux guichets, et les nombreuses enquêtes aux quelles l'administration a dû se livrer à la suite de potins, de cancans et de scandales, dans différents bureaux, viennent de déterminer la Direction Générale des Postes à suspendre pour quelque temps l'oeuvre immorale et dissolvante de la féminisation des bureaux de poste de Paris et de province . . ." The rumor regarding the suspension was unfounded, though *petite République* eventually got its wish.

25. Millerand, "Rapport sur le service des Postes," *Journal officiel,* 12 mai 1900, pp. 22-23.

26. *La Revue des Postes* 26 (17 décembre 1902): 1; Collet, *Des conditions du travail,* pp. 35-36; BPT TG1, Herman, "Ecole Professionnelle Supérieure des Postes et des Télégraphes. Législation et Exploitation Postales, session 1901-1902, mss.," pp. 92-94.

27. *Annuaire des Postes, 1909.* This was true even though the establishment of ten new post offices between 1900 and 1909 had provided the opportunity to use female employees without displacing men; women were introduced into only two of these ten bureaus. The major exception to the end of new feminizations was in colonized Algeria, as reported in *L'Union des Dames de la Poste* 5 (février 1904):11 and *Bulletin officiel de l'association générale des agents des P.T.T.* 3 (12 décembre 1903):334-35.

28. See, for example, Sembat, CDRCB, Exercise 1904, Impression No. 1206 (Paris, 1903), p. 115; Sembat, CDRCB, Exercise 1905, Impression No. 1956 (Paris, 1904), p. 249.

Chapter Six

1. Compare *Mémoire adressé au Parlement et à la presse par les dames de la Poste, du Télégraphe, du Téléphone et de la Caisse nationale d'épargne* (Paris, 1903), pp. 17-21; and Callet et du Grannut, *Place aux femmes* (Paris, 1973), pp. 27-30.

2. As portrayed in Paul Voucet, *Mademoiselle Téléphone* (Troyes, 1903).

3. Dalimier, CDRCB, Exercise 1914, Impression No. 3519 (Paris, 1913), pp. 122, 127.

4. Louis Figuier, *Le Téléphone, Son Histoire, Sa Description, Ses Usages,* (Paris, 1885), pp. 237-41; Brault, *Histoire de le Téléphone en 1888* (Paris, 1888), pp. 68-71.

5. *La Revue des Postes* 15 (9 septembre 1891):286-87. For later statistics see Sembat, CDRCB, Exercise 1906, Impression No. 2672 (Paris, 1905), pp. 151-53.

6. Sembat, CDRCB, Exercise 1902, Impression No. 2655 (Paris, 1901), pp. 86-89; Association générale des Agents, *Rapport sur la 'crise' des P.T.T.,* septembre 1905, p. 6.

7. Jacques Attali and Yves Stourdze, "The Birth of the Telephone and Economic Crisis," in *The Social Impact of the Telephone,* ed. de Sola Pool, pp. 97-111.

8. Quoted in *Le Journal des Postes et des Télégraphes* 16 (1 janvier 1893).

9. Alec Mellor, *La Fabuleuse Aventure du Téléphone* (Paris, 1975), pp. 66-68.

10. Musée de la Poste, Dossier Télécommunications.

11. BMD DOS/331/POS, 1899-1900.

12. Ibid. For background on Séverine, see Evelyne Le Garrec, *Séverine, une rebelle, 1855-1929* (Paris, 1982).

13. Sembat, CDRCB, Exercise 1905, p. 49; and Musée de la Poste, Dossier Télécommunications.

14. *Le Journal des Postes et des Télégraphes* 28 (2 juillet 1905).

15. *Le Matin,* 18 mars 1909. See Chapter 7 for a discussion of the strike.

16. Sembat, CDRCB, Exercise 1902, pp. 62-63; Sembat, CDRCB, Exercise 1903, Impression No. 616 (Paris, 1902), pp. 126-27.

17. BPT, PB173, "Question des Aides," p. 362.

18. Emile Mazoyer, Albert Faure, Louis Naud, *La Poste, Le Télégraphe et le Téléphone* (Paris, 1905), pp. 876-83.
19. Kératry, *Rapport,* pp. 328-29.
20. *Le Progrès du Nord,* quoted in *Le Journal des Postes et des Télégraphes* 28 (26 mars 1905).
21. Capart, fils, *Maladies et Açcidents Professionnels des Téléphonistes* (Paris, 1911).
22. Marcel Proust, *A la recherche du temps perdu,* vol. 3 (Paris, 1954), pp. 99-102.
23. Musée de la Poste, Documents.
24. For a description, see Laurent, *Services postaux en 1913,* pp. 111-12.
25. Mazoyer *et al, La Poste, Le Télégraphe et le Téléphone,* pp. 11-12.
26. Kératry, *Rapport,* p.336.
27. *Bulletin officiel de l'Association générale des Agents* (hereafter cited as *Bulletin de l'A.G.)* 4(1904):130-31; *L'Union des P.T.T.* 16 (5 mai 1905):1-2. One *dame employée* had reported in 1892 the following fixed expenses excluding food: 240 francs for rent (one room and kitchen); 150 francs for clothes, shoes, hats; 45 francs for laundry; 96 francs for heat and lighting; 30 francs for gifts and other expenses [*La Revue des Postes* 16 (28 septembre 1892):306-07].
28. ADG 6P169, Letter, 29 avril 1900.
29. ADG 6P162.
30. ADG P175, Letter, 28 juin 1910. A still worse fate than Paris for southern women, like men, was to be sent to a bleak industrial city in the north, a fact administrators implicitly recognized when they sent employees to such locales as disciplinary measures (see employee records).
31. Kératry, *Rapport,* pp. 488, 334.
32. Claude Boutin et Jean François Loubière, "Contribution à l'étude des phénomènes migratoires des pays d'oc vers Paris (19ᵉ-20ᵉ)" (Mémoire de maîtrise, second cycle, Université de Paris VII, 1975).
33. *La Revue des Postes* 13 (20 novembre 1889):374; *Bulletin mensuel des Postes et des Télégraphes* 15 (décembre 1892):1322; *La Revue des Postes* 19 (27 mars 1895):97; Ibid. 20 (3 juin 1896):177; *La Poste* 3 (12 juillet 1903):1; *L'Union des Dames de la Poste* 8 (octobre 1907):8.
34. *L'Union des Dames de la Poste* 4 (octobre 1903):5-6;4 (novembre 1903):7; 5(mars 1904):9-10; *Le Courrier des Examens* 17 (10 juillet 1905):458; *La Revue des Postes* 26 (27 août 1902); Ibid. 27 (23 septembre 1903):1; 27(30 septembre 1903):1.
35. BPT PB173, "Question des Aides."
36. Dumont, CDRCB, Exercise 1910, Impression No. 2767 (Paris, 1909), p. 101, Appendix I; Compte-rendu de l'assemblée générale de l'Association générale des Agents, 1910, pp. 232-34. The use of auxiliary telephone operators became important in the 1920s with the introduction of automatic telephone services, as they allowed more flexibility in reducing personnel [Dézarnaulds, CDRCB, Exercise 1928, Impression No. 4897 (Paris, 1927), p. 79].
37. *Bulletin mensuel des Postes et des Télégraphes* 26 (janvier 1903): 4. On women's role, see below, p. 106.
38. *Le Courrier des Examens* 13 (25 avril 1901): 263; *La Revue des Postes* 31 (16 février 1907): 2.
39. Kératry, *Rapport,* pp. 320-22, 334-35. Post office employees proper worked eight hour days, sometimes in split shifts.
40. Sembat, CDRCB, Exercise 1902, pp. 224-71. According to the report of a Dr. Minot, who had been commissioned to find practical means of combating the propagation of tuberculosis in the administration, of a group of 1,500 postal employees in the department of the Seine in 1899, 43 died from and 50 employees left the work force with T.B. The mortality rate from T.B. in Paris for the general population was 49/10,000. The Minister of Commerce and Posts intituted, in 1900, a committee to study the means of establishing a sanitorium for postal personnel.
41. *Annuaire des Postes, 1909.*

42. The statistical analysis here and below for *dames employées'* career patterns is based on a 10 percent sample of the work records of all *dames employées* born before 1876 in the provinces (the real number of whom was roughly 5,763) and of all work records of women born in Paris (who numbered approximately 1,115). These records show that about 52 percent of provincial-born women and 44 percent of Parisians reached retirement; owing to under-reporting, the real number in each instance was somewhat higher. The figures for men are based on a sample of approximately 725 clerks born 1859–1870, a group representing about 7 percent of the total.
43. Lange, *Au Service du Public,* pp. 13–14.
44. *Petit Parisien,* 18 mars 1909; *Le Journal des Postes et des Télégraphes 16* (23 avril 1893).
45. BPT PB173, "Question des Aides." Dumont, CDRCB, Exercise 1911, Impression No. 381 (Paris, 1910), p. 310 shows that of all women admitted to P.T.T. employment between 1904 and 1909, 79 percent had been *aides.*

Chapter Seven

1. *Le Journal des Postes et des Télégraphes* 8 (15 août 1885).
2. Ibid. 23 (2 octobre 1900).
3. Ibid. 23 (11 novembre 1900).
4. Ibid. 23 (28 octobre 1900).
5. *La Revue des Postes* 13 (2 janvier 1889):6; 16 (2 mars 1892):69; 17 (8 mars 1893):79; 32: 956 (16 février 1908):2.
6. *Le Journal des Postes et des Télégraphes* 23 (19 avril 1900); 23 (30 septembre 1900).
7. *Bulletin de l'A.G.,* avril 1901, pp. 38, 1.
8. *L'Union des P.T.T.* 13 (5 mai 1902):2.
9. "Propagande auprès des receveuses des bureaux simples et des dames employées," *Bulletin de l'A.G.* 1 (juin 1901):68–69; 2 (octobre 1902):164–66; 2 (1 juin 1902):1; Laurent, *Les services postaux en 1913,* pp. 403–04.
10. *L'Union des Dames de la Poste* (hereafter cited as *L'Union des Dames)* 4 (1 janvier 1903):1; 1 (1 octobre 1900):56.
11. Ibid. 4 (1 janvier 1903):1; 4 (juillet 1903):3.
12. Ibid. 3 (1 novembre 1902):1; 4 (1 juillet 1903):2; 3 (1 novembre 1902):3; 3 (1 décembre 1902):2; 4 (5 mai 1903):2.
13. BMD DOS/CON/FEM, "Rapports, Congrès du Travail Féminin, 1907" (correspondence of Durand). For clippings from *La Fronde* regarding women's employment in the P.T.T., see DOS/331/POS, DOS/350/FON.
14. *L'Union des Dames* 3 (15 décembre 1902):1; "Une carrière féminine," Ibid. 4 (1 mars 1903):1.
15. Madeleine Carlier, "Femmes fonctionnaires," *Le Journal des Femmes* 10 (août-septembre 1901):3; 11 (juillet 1902):4; (4 août 1902):4.
16. Arialy, "Le Féminisme et le Code Civile," *L'Union des Dames* 5 (octobre 1904):11–12; "Le Droit de Vote," Ibid. 8 (juin-juillet 1907):4–5.
17. *Le Journal des Postes et des Télégraphes* 28 (5 mars 1905).
18. Taïeb, *Hubertine Auclert,* p. 44.
19. Albert Dauzat, *La Liberté,* quoted in *L'Union des Dames* 6 (juin 1905):14; *La Poste* 3 (11 octobre 1903):1.
20. *L'Union des Dames* 5 (avril 1904):1; *La Poste,* 11 octobre 1903.
21. "Compte-rendu de l'assemblée générale de l'A.G., 1902" pp. 121–23, 278.
22. *Mémoire adressé au Parlement et à la Presse,* pp. 5–6.
23. Ibid., pp. 9–12.
24. *Bulletin de l'A.G.* 3 (mars 1903):63–64.
25. "Compte-rendu de l'assemblée générale de l'A.G., 1903," pp. 17–18.
26. Ibid., pp. 45ff.

27. *L'Union des Dames* 4 (novembre 1903):2.
28. Ibid.
29. Official membership figures given by the A.G. were 12,582 (1905); 1,329 (1906), 13,162 (1907); 12,757 (1908); 13,462 (1909). Considering that the number of employees was rising every year, the stagnation in enrollment is striking.
30. *Le Courrier des Examens* 17 (9 novembre 1905):708–14.
31. PP BA1437, 9 octobre 1906.
32. *Bulletin de l'A.G.* 4 (juin 1904):180. There were 7,276 clerks and apprentice clerks *(surnuméraires)* in the A.G. the same year. The remaining members included 750 chief clerks and heads of ambulatory brigades, and other scattered categories of personnel up to the higher ranks of departmental director.
33. "Compte-rendu de l'assemblée générale de l'A.G., 1903–1909;" *Bulletin de l'A.G.,* novembre 1905, p. 59; "Compte-rendu de l'assemblée générale de l'A.G., 1907."
34. Ibid., 1904, pp. 86–88; 1909, pp. 203ff.
35. *Journal officiel,* Débats de la Chambre des députés, 25–26 novembre 1903, comment of Rouanet; compare Chautard, CDRCB, Exercise 1909, Impression No. 2032 (Paris, 1908), pp. 58–60.
36. "L'Egalité," *L'Union des Dames* 9 (février 1908):2.
37. Under the name of "Zette," *Le Professionnel* 7 (15 octobre 1908):3–4.
38. *L'Union des Dames* 2 (20 août 1901):221–22; 3 (15 novembre 1902):1; 5 (juin 1904):4–5; 4 (15 mars 1903):1; janvier 1906, pp. 3–4.
39. Ibid. (septembre 1900):36.
40. Laurent, *Les services postaux en 1913,* pp. 477–514 provides a detailed chronology of the strike. See also, Danielle Tartakowski, "La Grève des postiers de 1909" (Mémoire de Maîtrise, Sorbonne, 1969).
41. Although the cost of living allowance rose between 1902 and 1909 by 150 francs for clerks and *dames employées* in Paris, the increase, which brought the total allowance to 400 francs, was insufficient to cover increased expenses and inferior to the cost of living allowance granted other Parisian civil servants. [Dalimier, CDRCB, Exercise 1912, Impression No. 1258 (Paris, 1911), pp. 365–370.]
42. Dalimier, CDRCB, Exercise 1913, Impression No. 1894 (Paris, 1912), Annexe VI.
43. Percentages based on *concours* results announced in *Journal officiel,* lois et décrets, 25 novembre 1909, 29 août 1909, 24 août 1910, 18 février 1911. Earlier percentages, based on birthplaces found on employee records, show that the recruitment of *aides* as *dames employées* in the 1890s as well as the opening of jobs for women in provincial cities had widened the geographical base of national recruitment. Of 6,861 women born before 1876, 25 percent had come from the southwest (see Chapter 3, note 14 for departments). Of 9,885 men born 1859–1870, 34.8 percent were from this same region. Since employee records do not reflect the migration out of a department or region after birth, the actual increase by 1909 may have been greater than shown in the *concours* results, which list the department where the candidate resided at the time of the examination. In any case, these comparative figures for men and women over time suggest that there was a time lag of a decade or two between recruitment patterns for men and women, but that in many respects the trend was similar. Michel Crozier made a similar observation in his study of civil servants included in *The Bureaucratic Phenomenon,* (Chicago, 1963), pp. 16–17. See also, Michel Crozier, *Petites fonctionnaires au Travail* (Paris, 1956).
44. BPT PB173, "Question des Aides," pp. 10, 46, 92–93, 296–97.
45. Thus, whereas profits rose sharply between 1901 and 1905, reaching a previously unsurpassed 91.7 million francs, net revenues fell off after 1905 so that in 1909 the profits accrued were at a pre-war low of 44.3 million francs (Dalimier, Exercise 1913, Annexe VI).
46. Laurent, *Les services postaux en 1913,* pp. 477–82.
47. PP BA1391, 17 mars 1909.
48. *L'Illustration,* 20 mars 1909.
49. PP BA1391, 17 mars 1909, A.G. strike poster, "La grève des postiers à l'opinion publi-

que''; *La Révolution,* 15 mars 1909; *Le Temps,* 16 mars 1909, 17 mars 1909; *Le Soleil,* 16 mars 1909; *Le Journal,* 16 mars 1909; *Petit Parisien,* 17 mars 1909.

50. Army troops were brought in to guard postal, telephone, and telegraph bureaus as well as to intimidate employees from joining the strike.
51. *Le Matin,* 17 mars 1909; ADN M623, Grèves, Postes, 1909; ADPC M1791, Grèves des P.T.T., 1909.
52. *Le Matin,* 18 mars 1909.
53. *Le Journal,* 18 mars 1909.
54. *Le Journal des Femmes* 18 (avril 1909):4; *Le Professionnel* 8 (15 juin 1909):2.
55. "Compte-rendu de l'assemblée générale de l'A.G., 1913," pp. 96–97.
56. See, for example, "L'Accession des Dames à l'Emploi de Rédacteur," *Bulletin Officiel de l'A.G.* 12 (mars 1912):104–05; and *Le Professionnel* 11 (15 novembre 1912):3; Compte-rendu de l'assemblée générale, 1913, p. 99.

Conclusion

1. In an interview in the fall, 1978, Mme Perret, who began work as a telephone employee during World War One, described the many branches of her family of *postiers.* She spoke fondly of her husband, himself a *postier* whom she had met soon after entering employment but who soon departed for the front. Fortunately he returned. Mme Perret made clear that she and her husband were and would continue to be (until her death in 1981) "copains." They were both union militants and during their forced absence from the work force in 1934—when they were fired for their role in strike activities—they spent the year happily together "fishing and bicycling."
2. Varenne, CDRCB, Exercise 1918, Impression no. 4131 (Paris, 1917), pp. 16–20, 71–72. For descriptions of *receveuses* who were war heroines in the war of 1914-1918 and that of 1870, see Bouvier, *Histoire des dames employées,* pp. 322–53.
3. Lafont, CDRCB, Exercise 1929, Impression no. 633 (Paris, 1928), pp. 53–54; Lafont, CDRCB, Exercise 1930, Impression no. 2274 (Paris, 1929), pp. 222–24; Lafont, CDRCB, Exercise 1931-1932, Impression no. 3885 (Paris, 1930), Tome II, pp. 33, 96–97, 105–06; Dezarnaulds, CDRCB, Exercise 1927, Impression no. 3413 (Paris, 1926), pp. 29–32, 62. See BMD, DOS/331/POS for clippings on telephone employees' actions on the equal pay issue.
4. Geneviève M. Bécane-Pascaud, *Les Femmes dans la Fonction Publique,* Notes et Etudes Documentaires, nos. 4056–4057 (Paris, 1974); Secrétariat d'état aux postes et télécommunications, direction du personnel et des affaires sociales, *Statistiques du personnel* (Paris, 1975).

Bibliography

Archives

Archives Nationales:
  A$\underline{S}$—*Archives des Associations*
  F^7—*Police*
  F^{12}—*Commerce et Industrie*
  F^{90}—*Postes et Télégraphes*
Archives Départementales du Calvados, de la Gironde, du Hérault, du Nord, du Pas-de-Calais, de la Seine-et-Marne, du Yvelines et de l'Ancien Département de Seine-et-Oise:
  Séries M—Personnel, Police, Administration générale
  Séries P—Postes et Télégraphes
  Etat Civil—Actes de Naissance, 1835-1875 (Gironde, Hérault, Nord)
Archives de Paris et de l'Ancien Département de la Seine:
  Dénombrement de la population, banlieue, 1891, 1896, 1911
  Etat Civil—Actes de Naissance, 1835-1870, Régistre des Mariages
  Listes électorales
Mairies de Paris: Etat Civil—Actes de Naissance, 1871-1875
Ministère des Postes et des Télécommunications, Feuilles de Personnel
  (employee records for women born 1871-1875)
Musée de la Poste (Paris)
Bibliothèque du Ministère des Postes et des Télécommunications
Bibliothèque Marguerite Durand (Paris)
Préfecture de Police (Paris)

Periodicals (Postal employees) (Abbreviations in parentheses indicate where materials may be found.)

L'Administration des P.T.T., 1901-1909 (BN)
Le Bulletin Hebdomadaire des P.T.T., 1896-1906 (BPT)
Le Courrier des Examens des Postes et des Télégraphes, 1889-1914 (BPT)
Le Journal des Postes (later *Le Journal des P.T.T.*), 1878-1900 (BN)
Le Moniteur des P.T.T., 1890-1893 (BN)
La Poste, 1901-1903 (BN)
Le Professionnel des P.T.T., 1902-1917 (BN)
La Revue des Postes (later: *La Revue des P.T.T.*), 1877-1914 (BN)
L'Union des Dames de la Poste (later: . . . *des P.T.T.*), 1900-1907 (BPT)
L'Union des P.T.T., 1892-1906 (BN)

Other Periodicals

La France Administrative, 1840-1846 (BN)
La Française, 1906-1907 (BN)
La Gazette des Femmes, 1840-1845 (BN)

L'Illustration, 1878-1914
Le Journal des Femmes, 1891-1911 (BN)
La Petite République, 1892-1894

Printed Materials

Compte-rendu de l'assemblée générale de l'Association générale des Agents des P.T.T.,
1901-1914, 1919 (AN, BPT).
Bulletin officiel de l'Association générale, 1900-1914 (BPT).
Mémoire adressé au Parlement et à la presse par les dames de la Poste, du Télégraphe,
du Téléphone et de la Caisse nationale d'épargne, 1903 (BPT).

Unless otherwise noted, the works listed below were published in Paris.

Published Government Sources

Almanach Royal. 1785-1793.
Annuaire des Postes (later: *Annuaire des P.T.T.*). 1808-1877 (intermittently), 1878-1909.
Bulletin mensuel de l'Administration des Postes (later: . . . *des P.T.T.*). 1855-1914.
Cochery, Adolphe. *Rapport présenté à M. le Président de la République.* 1884.
Direction Générale des Postes et Télégraphes. *Rapport présenté à M. Siegfried, Ministre*
du Commerce et de l'Industrie, par M. J. de Selves, directeur général des postes et des
télégraphes, sur les améliorations apportées dans le service depuis le 1er janvier 1890
jusqu'à la fin de décembre 1892.
Instruction générale sur le service des Postes (later: . . . *des P.T.T.*). 1792, 1806, 1832,
1856, 1868, 1876, 1899, 1904, 1915.
Kératry (de). *Rapport présenté à la Commission extra-parlementaire des Postes et des*
Télégraphes. 1911.
Ministère des Postes et des Télégraphes (later: Ministère des Finances, then Ministère
du Commerce, de l'Industrie, des Postes et . . . , then Ministère des Travaux Publics,
des Postes et . . .). *Compte définitif des dépenses de l'exercice, 1878-1914.* 1879-1915.
"Rapport au President de la République sur les conditions du fonctionnement de
l'Administration des Postes et des Télégraphes." *Journal Officiel,* 2 mai 1900 (Millerand
report).
Rapport fait au nom de la Commission du budget chargée d'examiner le projet de loi portant
fixation du budget général (Services des Postes et des Télégraphes), de l'exercice
1878-1932. 1877-1931. (For individual authors who headed the committees and printed
impression numbers, see notes.)
Riant, Léon. *Rapport sur l'Administration des Postes présenté au Ministre des Finances.*
Octobre 1877.
Vandal, Ed. *Rapport du 21 novembre 1864 au Ministre des Finances.* 1865.
————. *Rapport du Ministre des Finances sur le service des Postes,* janvier 1866. 1866.

Books by Contemporaries

Association des Abonnés du Téléphone. *Téléphones, Postes, et Télégraphes, Renseignements*
pratiques. La Rochelle, 1911.
Bachéré, J. B. *Racueil de correspondances à l'usage des Directions des postes et des*
télégraphes. Rennes, 1894.
Barnier, A. *Manuel des postulants aux recettes de début et aux emplois de dames dans*
le service des Postes et des Télégraphes. Digne, 1891.

Susan Bachrach

Bastien, P. *Les carrières de la jeune fille*, 1903.

Belloc, Alexis. *Les Postes Françaises*. 1886.

—————. *La Télégraphie historique depuis les temps les plus reculées jusqu'à nos jours*. 1888.

Berthet, Elie. *La Directrice des Postes*. 1861.

Block, Maurice. *Dictionnaire de l'administration française*. 2nd ed. 1878.

Bonnefoy, Antoine. *Place aux femmes: les carrières féminines administratives et libérales*. 1914.

Bonneff, L. *La Classe Ouvrière*. 1910.

Borrel, J.G. *Guide pratique des candidats aux emplois de surnuméraires, commis auxiliaires, de dames télégraphistes et téléphonistes*. 1884.

—————. *Les Recettes Simples (Bureaux de Début): Conseils aux candidates, aux aides et aux receveuses*. 1886.

Brasier, Léon. *Histoire des Maisons d'Education de la Légion d'Honneur*. 1912.

Brault. *Histoire de le Téléphone en 1888*. 1888.

Capus, Alfred. *Le personnel féminin des P.T.T. pendant la guerre*. 1915.

—————. *La petite fonctionnaire*. 1904.

Charton, Edouard. *Dictionnaire des Professions*. 3rd ed. 1880.

Chauvin, Jeanne. *Etude historique sur les professions accessibles aux femmes*. 1892.

Cim, Albert. *Bureaux et Bureaucrates, mémoires d'un employé des P.T.T.* 1910.

—————. *Demoiselles à Marier*. 1894.

Collet, Ludger. *Des conditions du travail dans l'Administration des Postes et Télégraphes*. 1910.

Daubié, Julie. *La Femme pauvre au XIXᵉ siècle*. 1866.

Duchesne, Léon. *Hygiène Générale et Hygiène Industrielle*. 1896.

n.a. "The employment of women in the postal service." *L'Union Postale Internationale*. Berne, 1 December 1876.

Figuier, Louis. *Le Téléphone. Son Histoire, sa Description, ses usages*. 1885.

Frank, Louis. *La femme dans les emplois publics*. Bruxelles, 1893.

Gibon, Fénelon. *Employées et ouvrières. Conditions d'admission et d'apprentissage, emplois, traitements, salaires*. Lyon, 1906.

Haussonville, Compte d'. *Salaires et misères de femmes*. 1900.

Issanchou, Henri. *Le livre d'or des Postes*. 1885.

Jaccottey, Paul. *Traité de Législation et d'exploitation postales*. 1891.

Lange, S. de. *Au Service du Public durant quarante ans 1887-1926*. Lyon, 1929.

Laurent, Benjamin. *Poste et postiers*. 1922.

—————. *Services postaux en 1913. L'organisation administrative, le syndicalisme postal*. Saint-Etienne, 1913.

Lavesvre, Emile. *Nos Télégraphistes, moeurs de la vie de bureau*. Montauban, 1888.

Lecomte, Georges. *Les cartons verts, romain contemporain*. 1901.

Legouvé, Ernest. *La Femme en France au XIXᵉ Siècle*. 1873.

Leroy-Beaulieu, Paul. *Le Travail des Femmes au XIXᵉ siècle*. 1873.

Lemaire, Charles. *Télégraphes. Conférence destinée aux dames*. 1878.

Mazoyer, Emile and Albert Faure, Louis Naud. *La Poste, Le Télégraphe, et Le Téléphone*. 1905.

Miret, Victor. *Essai sur la sociologie à propos de la protestation des employés des postes, des télégraphes et des chemins de fer*. 1888.

Ostrogorski, M. *La femme au point de vue de droit public*. 1892.

Regnal, Georges. *Comment la femme peut gagner sa vie*. 1908.

Réval, Gabrielle. *L'Avenir de nos filles*. 1904.

Ribouthet, G. *Le personnel des Postes et des Télégraphes*. Rennes, 1896.

Rouyer, Camille. *La Femme dans l'Administration. Tours, 1900*.

Roy, J. J. *La Directrice de Poste*. Tours, 1894.

Simon, Jules. *L'Ouvrière*. 1861.

Toulon, François. *Les Professions des femmes*. 1909.

Telrouc. *Boutades postales.* 1873.
Ulliac-Trêmadeure, Sophie. *Souvenirs d'une vieille Femme,* 1861.
Vaughan, E. *Maison Cochery et Cie. Postes et Télégraphes.* 1883.
Voucet, Paul. *Mademoiselle Téléphone.* Troyes, 1903.

Secondary Sources

Albistur, Maïté and Daniel Armogathe. *Histoire du féminisme français.* 2 vols. 1977.
Anglade, Henri. *Trafic postal et cycle économique.* 1946.
Bardèche, M. *Histoire des Femmes.* 1968.
Bécane-Pascaud, Geneviève. "Les Femmes dans la Fonction Publique." *Notes et Etudes Documentaires (nos. 4056-4057).* 25 janvier 1974.
Berger, Ida. *Les Maternelles.* 1959.
Blaxall, Martha and Barbara Reagan, eds. *Women and the Workplace: The Implications of Occupational Segregation.* Chicago, 1976.
Bouvier, Jeanne. *Histoire des dames employées dans les P.T.T. de 1714 à 1929.* 1930.
Brunel, Georges. *La Poste à Paris.* Amiens, 1920.
Callet et du Grannut. *Place aux Femmes.* 1973.
Charrier, Edmée. *L'évolution intellectuelle féminine.* 1931.
Chevalier, O. "Une famille de postiers bisontins, 1760-1848." *Revue des P.T.T.* 19 (novembre-décembre 1964):28-31.
Crozier, Michel. *The Bureaucratic Phenomenon.* Chicago, 1963.
————. *Petites fonctionnaires au travail.* 1956.
————. *The World of the Office Worker.* Translated by David Landau. Chicago, 1971.
Cushing, Marshall. *The Story of Our Post Office.* Boston, 1893.
Davies, Margery. "Woman's Place is at the Typewriter: The Feminization of the Clerical Labor Force." *Radical America* 8 no. 4 (1974):1-28.
Encyclopédie des Postes, Télégraphes et Téléphones. Ouvrage publié avec la collaboration des fonctionnaires des P.T.T. 1957.
Frischmann, Georges. *Histoire de la Fédération C.G.T. des P.T.T.* 1967.
Garrison, Dee. "The Feminization of Public Librarianship." *Journal of Social History* 6, no. 2 (Winter 1972-73): 131-59.
Greenwald, Maureen. "Women Workers and World War I: The American Railroad Industry, a Case Study." *Journal of Social History* 9, no. 2 (1975):154-177.
Guilbert, Madeleine. "L'évolution des effectifs du travail féminin en France depuis 1866." *Revue française du Travail.* Septembre 1947.
————. *Les femmes et l'organisation syndicale avant 1914.* 1966.
————. *Fonctions des Femmes dans l'Industrie.* 1966.
Holcombe, Lee. *Victorian Ladies at Work: Middle-Class Working Women in England and Wales 1850-1914.* Hamden, Conn., 1973.
Kanipe, Esther S. "The Family, Private Property and the State in France, 1870-1914." Ph.D. dissertation, University of Wisconsin, 1976.
Le Garrec, Evelyne, *Séverine, une rebelle; 1855-1929.* 1982.
Mayeur, Françoise. *L'Education des Filles en France au XIXe siècle.* 1979.
Mellor, Alec. *La Fabuleuse Aventure du Téléphone.* 1975.
Meyers, Peter V. "From Conflict to Cooperation: Men and Women Teachers in the Belle Epoque." *Historical Reflections* 7, no. 2-3 (1980):493-505.
Miller, Michael B. *The Bon Marché.* Princeton, 1981.
Mythes et représentations de la Femme au dix-neuvième siècle. Dix-huit études pluridisciplinaires du numéro special de *romantisme.* 1976.
Oppenheimer, Valerie K. *The Female Labor Force in the U.S.* Berkeley, 1970..
Ouzouf, Jacques. *Nous les Maitres d'Ecole.* 1973.
Parent-Lardeur, Françoise. *Les Demoiselles de magasin.* 1970.
Pellégrin, M. "Pendant plus d'un siècle une seule famille a géré le bureau de Bourg

d'Oisans." *Revue des P.T.T.* 15 (mai–juin 1960):39-44.

Pool, Ithiel de Sola. *The Social Impact of the Telephone.* 1977.

Prost, Antoine. *Histoire de l'Enseignement en France 1800-1967.* *1968.*

Silver, Catherine. "Salon, foyer, bureau: women and the professions in France." *American Journal of Sociology* 78: 4 (1973): 836-51.

Sowerwine, Charles. "Women and Socialism in France, 1871-1921: Socialist Women's Groups from Léonie Rouzade to Louise Saumoneau," Ph.D. dissertation, University of Wisconsin-Madison, 1973.

Sullerot, Evelyne. *Histoire et Sociologie du Travail Féminin.* 1968.

Taïeb, Edith. *Hubertine Auclert, La Citoyenne, 1848-1914.* 1982.

Tartakowski, Danielle, "La Grève des Postiers de 1909." Mémoire de maîtrise, Sorbonne, 1969.

Thuillier, Guy. *La Vie Quotidienne dans les Ministères au XIXe Siècle.* 1976.

Tilly, Louise A. and Joan W. Scott. *Women, Work and Family.* New York, 1978.

Trempé, Rolande. "L'utilisation des archives d'entreprise: le fichier du personnel." *Mélanges d'Histoire Sociale offerts à Jean Maitron.* 1976, pp. 249-64.

Vaillé, Eugène. *Histoire des postes françaises.* 2 vols. 1946-1947.

Zylberberg-Hocquard, Marie-Hélène. *Féminisme et Syndicalisme en France.* 1978.

Index